Build Your

New House
...In No Time

Lon Safko

que®

800 East 96th Street,
Indianapolis, Indiana 46240

Build Your New House In No Time

Copyright © 2005 by Que Publishing

All rights reserved. No part of this book shall be reproduced, stored in a retrieval system, or transmitted by any means, electronic, mechanical, photocopying, recording, or otherwise, without written permission from the publisher. No patent liability is assumed with respect to the use of the information contained herein. Although every precaution has been taken in the preparation of this book, the publisher and author assume no responsibility for errors or omissions. Nor is any liability assumed for damages resulting from the use of the information contained herein.

International Standard Book Number: 0-7897-3456-7

Library of Congress Catalog Card Number: 2005928025

Printed in the United States of America

First Printing: October 2005

08   07   06   05   4   3   2   1

Trademarks

All terms mentioned in this book that are known to be trademarks or service marks have been appropriately capitalized. Que Publishing cannot attest to the accuracy of this information. Use of a term in this book should not be regarded as affecting the validity of any trademark or service mark.

Warning and Disclaimer

Every effort has been made to make this book as complete and as accurate as possible, but no warranty or fitness is implied. The information provided is on an "as is" basis. The author and the publisher shall have neither liability nor responsibility to any person or entity with respect to any loss or damages arising from the information contained in this book.

Bulk Sales

Que Publishing offers excellent discounts on this book when ordered in quantity for bulk purchases or special sales. For more information, please contact

U.S. Corporate and Government Sales
1-800-382-3419
corpsales@pearsontechgroup.com

For sales outside of the U.S., please contact

International Sales
international@pearsoned.com

Publisher
Paul Boger

Executive Editor
Candy Hall

Acquisitions Editor
Loretta Yates

Development Editor
Sean Dixon

Managing Editor
Charlotte Clapp

Project Editor
Mandie Frank

Copy Editor
Lisa Lord

Indexer
Ken Johnson

Proofreader
Suzanne Thomas

Technical Editor
Sherry Kemper

Publishing Coordinator
Cindy Teeters

Multimedia Developer
Dan Scherf

Designer
Anne Jones

Build Your New House ...In No Time

Contents at a Glance

Table of Contents

I What You Need to Know Before You Start to Build

II Getting Started

III Starting the Design Process

IV Planning and Prevention Will Build a Better Home

Appendixes

About the Author

Lon S. Safko started his career in the building industry in 1976 as a land surveyor. He graduated from Westchester College with an advanced degree in civil technology and started his own engineering company, Civil Consultants. Over the next several years, Lon expanded from land surveying into soil analysis, hydrologic studies, traffic analysis, earthwork computation, subdivision and shopping center design, highway design, topography, and cartography and eventually developed one of the first computer systems to perform computer-aided design (CAD) for engineering.

Lon has contributed his engineering talents to the world headquarters of IBM, Texaco, PepsiCo, Exxon Oil, General Foods, and even the historic Sleepy Hollow Cemetery. Lon also attended Mercy, Pace, and Hostra universities. He has supervised custom residential construction and is currently certified as a real estate instructor by the state of Arizona, where he teaches several classes to realtors and the public on new home construction.

Dedication

To the memory of Ed Willard, my grandfather, who was a carpenter who placed the first hammer in my hands, and Larry Willard, my uncle, who hired and inspired me to become a civil engineer.

Acknowledgments

I would like to sincerely thank the staff at Que Publishing, Candy, Sean, Mandie, and Lisa for the patience and skills to take a rough dream and turn it into this finished reality.

We Want to Hear from You!

As the reader of this book, *you* are our most important critic and commentator. We value your opinion and want to know what we're doing right, what we could do better, what areas you'd like to see us publish in, and any other words of wisdom you're willing to pass our way.

As the publisher for Que Publishing, I welcome your comments. You can email or write me directly to let me know what you did or didn't like about this book—as well as what we can do to make our books better.

Please note that I cannot help you with technical problems related to the topic of this book. We do have a User Services group, however, where I will forward specific technical questions related to the book.

When you write, please be sure to include this book's title and author as well as your name, email address, and phone number. I will carefully review your comments and share them with the author and editors who worked on the book.

Email: feedback@quepublishing.com

Mail: Paul Boger
Publisher
Que Publishing
800 East 96th Street
Indianapolis, IN 46240 USA

For more information about this book or another Que Publishing title, visit our website at www.quepublishing.com. Type the ISBN (excluding hyphens) or the title of a book in the Search field to find the page you're looking for.

The housing industry in the United States is thriving more than ever. Last year alone, more than 2,018,200 new single-family homes were built in the United States (source: http://www.census.gov/const/www/newresconstindex.html). Total construction spending exceeded $550,134,000,000 (source: http://www.census.gov/const/www/c30index.html). That's more than half a billion dollars. And the number of licensed realtors registered with the National Association of Realtors last spring broke 1,005,785 (source: http://www.realtor.org/PublicAffairsWeb.nsf/Pages/1MillionMembers?OpenDocument).

With this much activity and so many people buying, selling, and building new homes, there had to be a book about that process. As a business consultant, I was constantly asked questions such as "What do I have to know to have a new home built?" "What does it cost?" "How do I find a good builder, realtor, lender?" "Where do I find the land?" "Should I build, buy, or remodel?"

This book will answer almost every question you have. If you're going to buy, build, or remodel, you're going to need to do your "home" work. Reading this book will make you an educated consumer.

Introduction

Welcome to *Build Your New House In No Time!* Thank you for purchasing this book. Deciding to purchase this book is the first decision of nearly 5,000 decisions you'll make during the construction of your new home. Making the second decision—to build your new home—will set you on an exciting and challenging course. Reading this book will help ensure that your new home is one you'll cherish for a lifetime.

The Largest Investment in Your Life: Be an Educated Consumer!

Buying or building a new home will probably be the largest investment you ever make. According to the National Association of Realtors, the median price of an existing home in the United States for 2005 was $267,400 (source: http://www.census.gov/const/www/newressalesindex.html). That's more than a quarter of a million dollars, which is, for most people, a substantial investment. You probably wouldn't buy a new TV or car without researching the latest features, ratings, and prices. However, some people go out and buy or build a new home without any knowledge of what goes into the building process.

Is $128 per square foot a good price? What can you expect to pay per square foot for granite, tile, Corian, or Formica countertops? Who gets to pick the title company? What are contingencies, selects, colorizing, draws, standard options, or flatwork? Is it okay if your foundation and floor crack? How do you find a good general contractor? Should you have a binding arbitration clause in your contracts? Why?

Unless you can answer all these questions, you need to do a little "home" work and become an educated consumer. The information in this book is based on current research done with general contractors, subcontractors, lending institutions, title companies, and realtors in the building industry.

If you're buying a new home or are a lender, title agent, or realtor representing a buyer, you'll find the information here invaluable. Avoiding even one small error during the building or buying process can save you or your client 100 times the cost of this book.

Who Should Read This Book

If you're planning to buy a new production or spec home, have a new custom or semi-custom home built, or renovate or add on to an existing home—or if you're a realtor or broker selling new homes, a title company or an agent insuring new homes, or a lender lending capital for building new homes—you owe it to yourself, your family, and your company to read this book.

With more than 2,018,2,111,000 new single-family homes being built in the United States this year alone, total construction spending exceeding $550,134,000,000 (half a billion dollars), and the number of licensed realtors last spring breaking 1,005,785, you need to understand the building process (source: http://www.census.gov/const/www/newressalesindex.html).

How This Book Is Organized

This book takes you step by step through the process of buying a production or spec home, building a new custom or semi-custom home, or renovating or adding on to an existing home. Easy-to-follow chapters explain what you need to do and what you should expect from your contractor, subcontractors, and other professionals you have chosen. The book starts with helping you decide what's right for you—buying, building, or renovating—and helps you understand what you need to know before you start, during construction, and when your new home is finished.

How the Information Is Organized

This book is divided into four parts and 24 chapters that lead you through all the major steps you need to know about the homebuilding process.

Part I: What You Need to Know Before You Start to Build

Part II: Getting Started

Part III: Starting the Design Process

Part IV: Planning and Prevention Build a Better Home

Part I: What You Need to Know Before You Start to Build

Part I takes you through the decision process of what type of home is right for you: custom, semi-custom, or production. If you're just staying where you are and adding on or remodeling your existing home, this information also applies to your situation, but this book is mainly for people who are having a new home built from scratch. This book doesn't address homebuyers who want to become their own homebuilders. It's for those who will work with a professional homebuilder to get the home of their dreams.

After you know what you want to accomplish, this step is where you begin to build your team. You pick your lender, title agent, realtor, homebuilder, and some of your own subcontractors, such as installers for swimming pools and block fences and maybe your landscaper. Part I also explains a few simple methods for finding out whether your team members should be on your team at all. I discuss how to carry out due diligence on your team to be sure they are experienced, trustworthy, and financially secure.

These chapters also address questions such as How do I get prequalified? How do I choose a good realtor, title agent, and lender? Do I have enough insurance? After you've answered these questions and more, you'll be ready to start your project.

Part II: Getting Started

Part II is all about what you need to do before you begin building. It describes major decisions you need to make before you start to build momentum. Make these decisions upfront so that you won't be pressured when time has run out. Planning ahead in this way helps you make the right decisions so that you can avoid change orders, cost overruns, project delays, subcontractor travel fees, living with mistakes, and a lot of stress. Making these decisions eases the building process and results in the home you've always dreamed of.

Part III: Starting the Design Process

In Part III, I explain how much house can you buy or build or, as homebuilders call it, "dollars on the dirt." I discuss how to determine how much house you can get for your money and explain allowances, standard options, cost comparisons, and the three-bid kickback. All these items affect the quality of your new home.

Part IV: Planning and Prevention Build a Better Home

Part IV is where I actually "break ground" and discuss building your new home. I explain what you need to know about the actual building process from the foundation to the roof—or trees to keys. The steps in this process are what homebuilders supervise and coordinate with their subcontractors to complete your new home. Much of the information in Part IV describes what they do but is important for you to understand. Knowing what to expect and how the process works can eliminate a lot of misunderstandings, make the process more enjoyable, reduce mistakes, and possibly eliminate legal battles.

As you finish Part IV, you're in the finish line. These chapters discuss builder's checklists, walkthroughs, maintenance of your new home, home inspections, and the dreaded rights and recourse, just in case. When you're through with Part 4, you should be ready to start buying or building your new home or offering a higher level of customer service to your clients.

Additional Resources

When you purchase this book, you gain access to a multitude of support files that help you understand the processes of buying, building, and borrowing even better. To download the free bonus materials for this book, such as the New Home Ideas workbook and an extensive glossary of building terms, go to www. betterhomesseminars.com to register and receive your password.

- Sample Loan Application
- Sample Blueprints
- Sample Builder's Schedule
- Sample Walkthrough Checklist
- Sample Select Sheets
- Sample Change Order Sheet
- Property Interview Questions
- Home Maintenance Outline
- Sample Termite Inspection Report
- Termite Pretreatment Certificate
- Septic System Design and Permit
- Soil Compaction Report
- Home Inspection Report
- Building Permit Application

- Draw Schedule
- Loan Application (Quick App)

These documents can help you during the course of construction. I recommend filling them in and referring to them during the course of construction. They can assist you in decision making and help keep you from making errors and omitting important details that can be overlooked easily during the building project.

These documents are yours to keep. Just download them and keep them on your computer for reference and to complete as you prepare to buy or build your new home. Keep the originals in a safe folder while you use a copy of the file to experiment with and to fill in as you proceed though the chapters of this book.

Throughout the book, you'll refer to these documents when I ask you to do your "home" work. You'll need to research your personal preferences for materials and finishes; gather brochures, pricing, and other information; and add your decisions to these forms.

Special Elements and Icons

I've done my best to arrange the material in this book so that you can zero in on what you need. This book has several special elements to help you do that:

- *Tips* indicate fairly easy actions you can take that will save you lots of time, money, and frustration.
- *Cautions* warn you against potential pitfalls and show you how to avoid common problems.
- *Notes* give you a little extra information about the topic currently under discussion that's good to know. This information is not necessarily essential, but it can be useful and will generally make you more knowledgeable about the subject.
- *To Do lists* tell you everything you need to do to get a specific task done. Think of them as checklists to help you mark your progress.
- *In This Chapter lists* at the start of every chapter give you the main objectives each chapter will help you accomplish.

Special icons have also been used to assist you in avoiding errors, show you cost-savings ideas, offer additional information from the Internet, and supply definitions of terms. Here are the icons you'll see throughout the book:

- The Errors to Avoid icon marks text indicating areas where you can easily make mistakes or other items that can help you avoid errors. These mistakes can cost you money, time, aggravation, and potential legal problems.

- The Dollars on the Dirt icon alerts you to text about topics that can cost you or save you money. These icons point out where being an educated consumer helps you negotiate better, know what you should and should not pay for, and discover where you can save just because you know how.

- The Internet Information icon directs you to websites that will make the building process easier, provide valuable information, and help you make those continual decisions that affect your project.

- The Definition icon acts as a pause from the main flow of information to further explain a term or concept so that you can understand it better before moving on to new ideas.

Recommendations for Using This Book

Buying, building, or renovating your new home is an experience you'll never forget and is one that can go both ways. I'm sure you have heard people say that they have built a new home and would never, ever do that again. Others have a great time with little stress, end up with the home of their dreams, and would recommend the experience to others. The difference is that these others knew what to expect and what was expected of them, and they communicated. When you know what you're doing, every process goes more smoothly.

Read the book all the way through, and follow the instructions to complete your "home" work assignments. These assignments are one of the most important things you can do to prepare. Then skim the book a second time. During the course of construction, scan the pages that apply to that phase of preconstruction or construction again, making sure you're doing everything you need to do to understand the process and schedule and are fulfilling your requirements as the homebuyer.

Create a set of files, collect information, make phone calls, talk to experts, gather brochures, get prices, and roll up your sleeves and enjoy. When else are you going to spend a quarter to a half million dollars again? I know that if I were spending half a million dollars, I would do everything I could to guarantee I had fun doing it!

Some Tips Before You Start

Get a notepad, an accordion file, a pen or marker, a tape measure, a digital camera, and access to the Internet because as I ask questions in the upcoming chapters, you're going to start compiling everything you need to know about your new home. When you're done, you'll have the confidence to go out and build your team of professionals, and then have them build your dream home with as little stress and as much fun as possible.

Part 1

What you Need to Know Before You Start to Build

Making a Decision on What to Build

Deciding whether building is right for you is the first step in this process. Only you can decide what's right for you and your family. Do you want to design and have a contractor build your dream home from the ground up? Do you want to build your home yourself with your own hands? Will your new home be a custom home, a semi-custom home, or a production home? What are the pros and cons of each type? Which is right for you? You have a lot of questions to consider.

Take your time answering these questions. There's no rush, and a 30-year mortgage takes a long time to pay off. Speak with your spouse, your friends, your relatives, and your co-workers to find out what their experiences have been. Sit down with your financial advisor and ask what options are available to you. Armed with the information in this book, you'll have everything you need to launch into the project of building your new home with enthusiasm.

It's an exceptionally exciting time for real estate. Over the next 12 months, 1,186,000 new homes will be built in the United States. All the new homes built in this country fall into two major product categories: production or tract homes and custom or semi-custom homes. This chapter describes both types of homes so that you can see which one is right for you. I also talk about what a general contractor (GC) can do for you and how hiring a good GC can make homebuilding a snap. Time to get started!

Understanding the Pros and Cons of Custom Homebuilding

You need to evaluate the pros and cons when deciding whether to buy a production home or find a GC and build a custom or semi-custom home. Some of the advantages are obvious, but many are not.

As you would expect, an advantage of building your own home is that you have more control over the design elements of a custom or semi-custom home than you do over a production home. A disadvantage is that you need to participate in many more decisions when building your own home. Another advantage is that you can build exactly the house that fits your specific lifestyle and design tastes. On the other hand, the more decisions that have to be made, the more opportunity for something to go awry.

Defining Your Options

The best place to start is to identify the choices you have in building your new home. Each choice comes with its own advantages and disadvantages, which often come down to a balance of time, money, and the ability to make design selections. There are tradeoffs in all these factors. Moving in more quickly to a home that's nearly complete might cost you more and leave you fewer design options, and the reverse might be true with other homes. When you understand what the process is and then decide which options are right for you, any choice you make will be exciting and rewarding. The following sections explain the different types of new homes you can buy and build.

Custom Home

A *custom home* is the true definition of your "dream home." *Custom* means "made to order," built to your specifications and your designs. When you decide to purchase a custom home, you're actually contracting a homebuilder to build a new home to your exact specifications. Building a new custom-built home can be expensive, but it doesn't necessarily have to be.

> **note** The homebuilder is the person responsible for the construction of your new home. This person can be referred to by many names: homebuilder, builder, contractor, general contractor (GC). Generally, I refer to him as the homebuilder, even though any of these names are appropriate.

If you choose to build a custom home, you can design everything about the home: the architectural style, the number of stories, the square footage, the floor plan layout, the number and sizes of rooms, window and door positions, wall and floor treatments, closet sizes, and even quirky design elements, such as a meditation room on the roof (no kidding), dumbwaiters, and secret passages (really). I've seen all these unusual elements, and I can promise you, you won't get them in a production home. With a custom home, you control the complete design from the ground to the roof, from trees to keys.

Semi-Custom Home

With a *semi-custom home*, the home's layout has already been determined along with the number of stories, square footage, number of garage stalls (bays), position on the lot, and architectural style. Many homebuilders choose to build semi-custom homes because it's easier for them. Many homeowner decisions have been eliminated, thus reducing the possibility of errors and often difficult input from homeowners, and semi-custom homes follow plans that builders have used before and are comfortable with.

You can still have design input and choose your kitchen cabinets, floor coverings, paint colors, bathroom accessories, and even the electrical and plumbing fixtures.

SPEC HOMES

Another kind of home, similar to a semi-custom home, is a *spec home*. With this type of home, the homebuilder builds the majority of it before the homebuyer buys it and begins to have input. In many cases, a spec home is 70% to 80% complete when it's sold to you, the homebuyer. The primary difference between a semi-custom home and a spec home is that with the spec home, the homebuilder speculates that he will sell the home at the precise moment the home is ready, and he funds the construction costs up to that point.

For homeowners, two advantages of a semi-custom home are more possibility of variety in its architectural design than in most production homes, which can have as few as four different models; also, the home is nearly completed and can be occupied in a short time. In addition, you get to make many of the finishing design decisions, such as exterior colors, wall and floor treatments, electrical and plumbing fixtures, garage doors, kitchen cabinet hardware, and so on.

Of course, a disadvantage is that many architectural design choices have already been made for new home, such as the floor plan, square footage, room sizes, and ceiling heights.

Production Homes

Definition

Production homes are often called "tract" homes. Although production homes usually provide the most value, most people don't realize that if negotiated properly, the cost difference between a fully custom home and a production home can be quite small. The cost, of course, depends on the builder, the area, the current market, your ability to negotiate, and many other factors. So if you're on a tight budget, don't rule out a custom or semi-custom until you finish reading this book, and then meet with two or more custom/semi-custom homebuilders and negotiate a price per square foot. Check it out. You might be able to get a custom dream home for the cost of a tract home.

The advantages of production homes are numerous, which makes them the most popular new home choice in America today. They are well-constructed homes built by companies with good reputations; however, they offer a limited choice of predesigned floor plans and elevations. Production homes are usually built in planned communities ranging from 6 to 6,000 homes. Larger communities often include shopping centers, gas stations, cleaners, food stores, and even schools and churches. Having these conveniences can add a lot of value to your new home and convenience for you.

note Depending on your building market, a homebuilder might be willing to work with you on a tighter budget, include some items he might not normally include without additional charge, and generally quote you a lower per-square-foot cost for your new home. "Negotiating" refers to discussing the price per square foot, asking for those extras, and trying to get the best price for your new home.

Some homebuilders might include items such as textured walks, upgraded plumbing and electrical fixtures, 10-foot rather than 8-foot ceilings, a larger bathtub, bigger windows or an extra window, sliding glass doors, an extra garage door opener for the third stall, a larger hot water heater, a stone facade, pot shelves, designer wall switches and receptacles, and upgraded carpet. The standard upgrades they throw in are proportional to how much they want to close the deal.

Often production homes are mass-manufactured in a warehouse under strict specifications and quality control. These homes are built with the help of computerized milling and layout and are constructed in wall sections. After these sections are nailed together, they're loaded on a flatbed truck and driven to your lot location, often in another state. This home arrives at your site in numbered sections, is assembled on site, and then is finished according to the design of the specific neighborhood, subdivision, and builder.

Another pro is that this mass-manufacturing process reduces construction costs to the homebuilder, resulting in a good-quality home for a reasonable price with the added feature of neighborhood conveniences. The con? You can't change much, if anything. You can't move a wall, add a bathroom, or raise a ceiling. You get to pick out the carpet and paint, but the layout and architectural style have already been determined and are locked in.

Making the Right Choice for You

Before you make a decision on which type of new home is right for you, test-drive a few homes. Drive around your area and find one or two local custom homes. Meet with their builders and discuss your desires for a new home. Look at a few of the homes they built and get an idea what it would cost to build the home you've been thinking of.

> **note** Most production builders do give you a choice of kitchen cabinets, lighting and plumbing fixtures, roof tile, and other choices, although they're limited. The list of design elements you can pick from is called *standard options*. These items are generally of the same quality and differ only in style and color. For more information on standard options, see Chapter 11, "What You Need to Know About Standard Options."

Now test-drive a few production homes. They're easier to find and have a lot of choices in prices, floor plans, locations, and design. Speak with their sales agents to get an idea of their costs for what you might like to own.

Look at both neighborhoods and compare the newly developed neighborhood of the production homes to the more established areas of the custom builders. After you have done a little "home" work, you'll feel more comfortable about making the right decision for you, your family, your budget, and your future.

Reasons to Use a Homebuilder

A growing group of people think they could save a lot of money by being their own homebuilders. Can you really save money by going this route?

I hear people say, "It can't be that hard. A builder doesn't actually do any of the work. The subcontractors do it all, and I can keep the huge profit the builder would get!" My advice is "Please don't do that." Here are the four most important reasons not to become your own homebuilder:

- Homebuilders have the right relationships.
- Homebuilders understand the building process.
- Homebuilders can negotiate better prices.
- Homebuilders have the necessary insurances.

Homebuilders Have the Right Relationships

Most custom/semi-custom homebuilders have been building homes for most or all of their careers. In addition to building homes, they have been building relationships. It's who you know that makes all the difference, even in the building trade.

Homebuilders know who the good framers and good plumbers are. They also know who not to hire when building your new home. Your builder knows who to talk to in the city when something gets bogged down. He has most likely worked through situations similar to yours many times before and can expedite a solution. This is knowledge that can be learned only from years of experience, and often they learn it the hard way. Similar to hiring any professional, you're paying for their knowledge and experience.

Homebuilders Understand the Building Process

If I offered you a razor and a bottle of scotch, would you be willing to remove your own appendix? No, you wouldn't because you would die—you don't know what you're doing. You probably don't understand the intricacies of building an entire home, either. Even subcontractors don't know the entire process of building a home. A good homebuilder knows how to pick the right subcontractors (subs). He has established relationships with these subs, he knows how to communicate with them, he understands the jargon, he knows how to recognize problems before they occur, and he knows how to fix problems when they do occur. You might not have the necessary experience to do this, and learning how to solve these problems after they happen can be costly and time consuming.

Homebuilders Can Negotiate Better Prices

You can't negotiate the cost of labor and materials the way a homebuilder can. A homebuilder can negotiate a much better price than you can. Often subs and suppliers have relationships that go back 20 years or more. Subcontractors won't give you the same price for a plumbing package that they would give to a homebuilder for whom they have built 50 to 100 homes. When you go to a lumberyard, for example, to cost out your lumber package and ask for a bid price on building only one house, the price is much different than the price a homebuilder gets who walks into the same lumberyard and negotiates a price for 50 houses. Getting materials at wholesale discounted prices results in a larger margin between the homebuilder's costs and your cost of the finished home. This cost savings is what helps your homebuilder give you a better price on building your new home.

Homebuilders Have the Necessary Insurances

You don't have the necessary insurances. When homebuyers ask me, as a consultant, if they should become their own homebuilder, I tell them that if they pay for all the insurance they need, they can no longer afford to build their home. You need contractor's general liability, workman's compensation, and more. General liability alone can cost builders approximately $40,000 to $100,000, and without building experience or a state-issued homebuilder license, you probably couldn't even get it.

Workman's compensation can run as high as 150% of payroll costs, depending on the trade. Insurance is discussed more in Chapter 2, "Being Insured Properly Can Greatly Reduce Your Risk."

If You Must

Now, there are always people who, no matter what the risks or warnings, still want to build their own homes and become their own homebuilders. If you're one of these people, I recommend checking out several U.S. companies that can assist you in building your new home, new swimming pool, and more. These building-assist companies give you a free initial consultation, which usually includes a meeting to find out about your goals, project, and budget.

For example, UBuildIt is a building-assist company based in Kirkland, Washington. At the time of publication, it had 104 franchises throughout the United States, often associated with lumberyards or roof truss manufacturers. You can find them online at www.ubuildit.com.

These companies help you with your budget, your site evaluation, and plan development. They work with you to make sure you have the right lot and the right plans to meet your goals. They assist you in making sure the plans you pick meet your budget and lifestyle needs. They even review and evaluate your home-remodeling project.

After your plans are ready, they work with you to prepare costing specifications for each phase of the project. These specifications help subcontractors and suppliers give you accurate pricing and avoid omitting necessary items, which could create cost and schedule overruns.

Building-assist companies meet with you regularly to monitor your project's progress. They prepare construction calendars at each stage of your homebuilding or remodeling process, outlining the next tasks you need to perform. They also visit your site regularly and provide access to a select group of subcontractors. Some even give you 24-hour access to a building consultant. Generally, building-assist companies are paid between 8% and 9% of the total construction project cost.

> **caution** Traditionally, lenders don't finance owner-builder projects. Banks have often been reluctant to loan money to owner-builders because of uncertainty about their construction knowledge and skills and their ability to complete the project successfully. (There's a reason for that.) Often, if you work with one of these building-assist companies, lenders are more willing to grant loans for these projects.

Hiring a Homebuilder Takes the Pain Out of Homebuilding

I advise you to hire an experienced homebuilder to help you build your new house. Even though I discussed building-assist companies as an option in the previous section, I don't recommend going that way. If you have no experience with homebuilding, trying to be your own homebuilder can lead straight to mistakes you didn't see coming, higher costs, and needless frustration. I've already stated the best reasons for hiring a homebuilder, but now I want to go into more detail about what a good homebuilder can offer you.

Homebuilders Understand the Magnitude of the Project and Can Avoid Costly Errors

If you haven't built a house before, you probably don't have the experience to manage a project of this magnitude. When teaching classes on this subject matter, I tell students that even with my years of experience in commercial building and building residential homes, I still didn't have the experience to catch a simple error that cost a great deal of time and money to repair.

A while ago, I did some business consulting for a custom homebuilder, acting as his building superintendent on a residential subdivision construction site. We were building a Mission/Santa Fe–style home that was at the 75% construction phase; the home was nearly completed and needed only kitchen cabinets, finish mechanicals (lighting and pluming fixtures), and paint. The cabinetmaker came to the site to measure for the cabinets, when he notified me that he measured the opening for the refrigerator at 34 inches. The opening was between two wall partitions, as the homeowners didn't want to look at the side of the refrigerator against the end of the cabinets and counter or from the great room.

I had to admit to the cabinetmaker that I was puzzled why he was so concerned about the 34-inch dimension for the refrigerator. He then pointed out that the minimum opening had to be 36 inches for a refrigerator to fit. Oh, no! It was 2 inches too small. That meant we had to rip out the partition walls to accommodate the 36-inch opening. We had to rip out the framed and drywalled overhead soffits (where the cabinets attached to the ceiling) for the whole length of the counter along that wall in the kitchen. We had to tear up the floor tile around the walls to accommodate the walls' new positions. We had to relocate the electrical outlet for the countertop appliances and light switches. All that work meant demolition, framing, electrician, drywall, and texture subcontractors, not to mention the three weeks' delay to schedule and carry out these tasks.

The error? The framer didn't measure correctly. He missed a layout dimension and forgot to allow for the thickness of the drywall on both sides. It was a small error. The framer missed it and so did I. I'm glad the cabinetmaker caught it when he did, or we wouldn't have known about it until the homeowner tried to push the refrigerator into that opening on moving day. By the time the homeowner took possession of the home, the problem would have been even bigger. The custom cabinets would have been constructed and installed, the granite countertops would have been installed, and the homeowners would have been greatly inconvenienced by the demolition and reconstruction. The homebuilder's cost was considerable, but discovering this error later would have also cost him his reputation. This error and the subsequent remedy caused the end of a 10-year relationship between the homebuilder and his framer. Now, be honest. Did you know why 34 inches was so important when you first read this paragraph?

This story is only one example of the many things that can go wrong or be overlooked. Without years of experience in residential construction, you wouldn't be able to catch these errors, either. I've seen a home built one foot to the left of where it was supposed to go. This error made the home too close to a property line, which held up the Certificate of Occupancy for months while the homeowner pleaded with the local municipality to allow a zoning setback variance. The mistake wasn't obvious from the street.

I've seen footings poured out of square. Is this a big problem? Not for the framers because they framed to the foundation. When the home was 80% complete and it was time to install the tile in the kitchen/breakfast area, it was a problem, however. When the tile was installed, it was obvious that it didn't run parallel to the wall. On one end, the tile was tight; on the other end, the tile ran off 2 1/2 inches. It will be like that forever, and the homeowner has to look at this mistake every day.

It takes an experienced eye to catch all those mistakes and to prevent mistakes before they happen. That's why a homebuilder gets the big bucks—so that he can save big bucks for you. Remember, the home belongs to the homebuilder until it's finished and you decide to accept it. Until then, he's responsible for anything that goes wrong, and ultimately, it's his responsibility to correct anything that can go wrong. It's up to him whether he wants to fight with the responsible subcontactor or pay it himself. Either way, it's his responsibility to see that any problem gets fixed to your satisfaction. This is good to know! A good homebuilder's experience can also come in handy in a myriad of other areas, discussed in the following sections.

Material Delivery

Every single item for building a home needs to be listed, priced, ordered, delivered, and installed or assembled. Just knowing what all those items are is important. You can't miss a single item when building a home.

An experienced homebuilder knows where he can find the best quality at the best price and, equally as important, get the material to your job site on time. On time doesn't mean in time; it means on the exact day you need it. If the material arrives a day too soon, you have nowhere to store it safely and it might get stolen. If it arrives a day late, the subs will have already left your job and moved on to another. One day late on a material delivery can delay your project by a week or more. A homebuilderknows how to schedule material delivery and has relationships with the suppliers to get them to cooperate. A homebuilder's relationship with suppliers might result in warehousing your materials for longer than the suppliers wanted, unloading their delivery truck because your project is running a day behind, or making a special delivery to your job site. All this incurs additional expense for suppliers, which they are willing to accept because of the relationship they have with your builder.

SUBCONTRACTOR SCHEDULING

Timing is *everything*. A homebuilder is a master scheduler. He has relationships with both the subcontractors and the suppliers to coordinate them showing up together on your job site at exactly the right time. He also has the skills and leverage to get subcontractors to change their schedules if materials are delayed or back-ordered.

Municipality and Administrative Approvals

Building a home requires many approvals and permits. As with most governmental agencies, all the Ts' have to be crossed and all the I's have to be dotted. Five sets of plans must be submitted, not four. They have to be exactly 24×36 inches, not 18×24 inches. Your homebuilder knows all these details.

Often, unforeseen problems do arise during the permit process, and it's your homebuilder's relationships and experience that get them resolved quickly and with minimal expense. I consulted recently with a homebuilder who had trouble getting his subdivision approved because the county would not approve construction of the roads. The county tested the new roads in several areas and found the asphalt thickness a little less than required. This isn't a big problem from a construction perspective. When the top coat of asphalt is put down, it can be a little thicker than normal to compensate.

Here's the "however": The county can't approve the roads until the asphalt is the required thickness. Without the road approval, the subdivision can't be approved. Without the subdivision being approved, the town can't issue a Certificate of Occupancy (C of O), which allows a homeowner to occupy his or her new home. No C of O meant the homeowners of the three homes the builder had completed couldn't move in!

Because of the builder's relationships and, more important, his reputation with the county and town, he was given his C of Os because the officials knew the builder would correct the deficiency with the roads when the subdivision was finished. They trusted him based on past experience. This problem was solved with only a hand-shake.

Custom Manufacturing

Many items that go into your new home are manufactured off site, delivered, and installed at different stages of your home's construction. These items might include kitchen and bathroom cabinets, countertops, spiral staircase handrails, bathroom mirrors, front doors, fireplace surrounds, and more. Each item is hand-crafted to your and your builder's specifications.

Your homebuilder knows how to work with these craftspeople to get the quality you want and to get the work completed, delivered, and installed on time. With the current building boom in the United States, these craftspeople are under increasing pressure to meet tight construction schedules. Your builder has the ability to ask, say, your kitchen cabinetmaker to please stop working on another builder's projects and complete yours because your project is a week ahead of schedule. These skills have a great deal of value to you, the homebuyer.

Summary

This chapter has covered the pros and cons of each type of new housing solution so that you can understand your choices and better decide which is the right choice for you. You also learned about the importance of choosing a good homebuilder and why he can negotiate better prices, have the necessary experience to spot a problem before it becomes one, and work with the different municipalities to secure administrative approvals.

- Before you begin this process, understand your building options for a new home.

- Choose the type of new home that's right for you, your budget, your lifestyle, and your family.

- If you decide to build your new home yourself, do the necessary research so that you understand what support you'll get and what liability you might incur.

- Make a list of all the questions discussed in this chapter to ask your building-assist company so that you understand completely what your responsibilities are and what you can expect from the company.

Being Insured Properly Can Greatly Reduce Your Risk

Making sure that you and your homebuilder have the minimum required and, most important, adequate insurances is critical to the success and security of building your new home. Hundreds of thousands of new homes are built each year without a single incident, but as with all insurance, you want to be sure that if an incident happens to you, both you and your homebuilder are covered.

To do list

- ☐ Determine which of the two primary types of policies, standard homeowner's or dwelling and fire, is the best for you.
- ☐ Get your policy before your homebuilder begins construction.
- ☐ Reevaluate your coverage with your insurance agent when construction is complete, as your new home will be valued differently from your previous home.
- ☐ Speak with your homebuilder about the type and amount of insurance coverage he carries.
- ☐ Have your homebuilder's insurance company fax a copy of his certificate of insurance directly to you.

What Insurance Policies Do You Need While Building?

You can consider two primary types of policies for your new home while it's under construction: a standard homeowner's policy or a dwelling and fire policy.

What Exactly Do You Need to Be Safe?

You do need to consider homeowner's insurance for your new home during the course of construction. If you don't, you might be exposing yourself to a great deal of risk if a fire, theft, or other event damages or destroys your partially completed home, and your builder doesn't have adequate insurance or any insurance at all. During the course of construction, which generally can take seven to nine months, there's a possibility that your builder might let his insurance policies lapse. Even though this is rare, you should be prepared for this possibility. In "Why You Should Contact the Homebuilder's Insurance Company" later in this chapter, I'll show you how to be sure your homebuilder maintains active insurance policies and how to verify this over the course of construction.

One way to cover your new home during construction is by purchasing a *standard homeowner's policy*. This policy covers you for any

note Remember, the house itself doesn't become your property until you officially accept it at the time of closing. Until then, the homebuilder owns the home. This means your homebuilder is responsible for the structure, its contents, and any associated liability. If materials are stolen from the home or it's vandalized or burned down, your homebuilder is responsible for those losses. For this reason, many homebuilders don't allow you to store personal property in the home until the deed of trust is transferred to you.

damage to the building as it's being built and might also provide some coverage in the case of fire, lightning, wind storm, smoke, water damage, vandalism, glass breakage, and theft of building materials (although the contractor's insurance should cover material theft first). Also, coverage for earthquake and flood damage can usually be included for an additional cost.

A standard homeowner's policy also provides liability coverage, which can come in handy if a friend trips during a tour of your new dream home and decides to sue you for it. However, the policy doesn't cover your personal property until the building is secure—that is, has all its doors and windows and can be completely locked. When construction reaches this point, you can add homeowner's insurance coverage for your personal property.

Another option is to purchase a *dwelling and fire policy*. This type of policy does cover damage to the physical structure but provides no theft coverage. Again, this coverage is important if your homebuilder has let his policies lapse. A dwelling and fire policy might be an appropriate choice if you're living in your current home during the course of construction. A homeowner's policy on the house you're living in almost always covers theft of personal items from the construction site. Dwelling and fire policies also provide liability coverage, just as a standard homeowner's policy does.

After your new home is finished, you should sit down with your insurance agent and reevaluate your coverage. If you opted for dwelling and fire coverage, you might need to purchase a full homeowner's policy. If you bought a standard homeowner's policy, make sure you have purchased the right amount of insurance, especially if you have made alterations to the original building plans (such as adding on a room or upgrading flooring, electrical, and appliances). The best way to be sure is to meet with your homeowner's insurance agent to discuss your particular situation and take his or her advice.

If You Paid for the Insurance Your Builder Needs, You Could No Longer Afford to Build

Insurance cost is one of the primary reasons I recommend you choose to work with a reputable homebuilder, not build a home yourself. Being the primary insurance holder is expensive when you pay off all the insurances you need. When I teach this subject in my realtor classes, I advise students that if their clients paid for all the insurance they need, they could no longer afford to build their homes. It's better to use a homebuilder who has all the proper insurances and consider only supplemental coverage that can be added to an existing homeowner's insurance policy. The cost of protection is much lower than the cost of being without. Even if your homebuilder does have valid insurances in place, don't rely on it. A homebuilder might have adequate insurance, but does every one of your homebuilder's subcontractors have adequate and valid insurance?

You can purchase supplemental insurance policies for a fraction of the cost of being the primary insured for a minimum of 4 months and a maximum of 12. Extensions on the policies are available if your policy runs out because of a delay. The cost depends on the completed value of the home, the coverage selected, and length of time estimated until completion of construction. Because of the exposure to liability, it's important that coverage be put in place on the home and property as soon as you start working on the property, regardless of whether the foundation or framing has started.

> **note** A typical example of the kind of claim you might encounter is a homeowner who has several trees removed before signing with a homebuilder and discovers later that some of the trees were on neighboring property. The homeowner is responsible for paying the neighbor several thousand dollars for the value of the trees that were removed in error.

What Will the Necessary Protection Cost You?

The cost of rehabilitation in today's health care industry is staggering. As a consultant, I pose this question: "What if, say, a roofer fell off your roof and broke his neck while installing your roof tile? How much do you think it would cost and who is going to pay?"

The answer to the first question might surprise you. If a roofer fell on your construction site and was paralyzed from the neck down, the cost to save and rehabilitate that person during only the first five years after the accident is, on average, $3.2 million. What happens next? First, the roofer sues his employer, the subcontractor. Then he sues the homebuilder. Then he sues you. In this litigious society, it's better to just sue everyone and let the courts sort it out later.

Most insurance policies "cap out" (run out) at $1 million, so for the roofer in this example, you need 3.2 policies (or one big one). You might not think it's fair, but that's what happens if the sub or homebuilder doesn't have insurance or doesn't have adequate insurance. The courts start with his employer, the subcontractor's insurance company, and then move up to the homebuilder's insurance company. If those policies are inadequate, they come after you. Then there's the possibility that you just built your new custom home for that roofer, or worse. It pays to research everyone's insurance, including your own.

In almost every case, your homebuilder does have the proper insurances. I mention this only to encourage you to actually check to see that he does. If your homebuilder has the proper insurances and your homeowner's policy agent has advised you about supplemental insurance coverage, you now have the best of both worlds: all the protection you need at the minimum expense.

To do list

❑ Contact your homebuilder's insurance companies and have them fax you copies of the following certificates, all of which the homebuilder should have:

- General liability insurance
- Builder's risk insurance
- Workman's compensation insurance (workman's comp)

❑ Request that your homebuilder add you to his insurance policy as an "additional insured."

What Insurance Does a General Contractor Carry?

Homebuilders carry a wide range of insurance, depending on their expertise and specific area of construction. These insurances can include the following:

- *General liability*   Covers your homebuilder against accidents and injury that result in bodily injury or property damage to a third party; also covers the cost of defending lawsuits and any bonds or judgments required during an appeal procedure.

- *Builder's risk*   Also called course of construction insurance, covers your home while construction is in progress.

- *Contract surety bonds*   Protect you from financial loss in the event of contract failure by your homebuilder.

- *Errors and omissions policies*   Covers your homebuilder if a mistake happens or an error is caused by an important piece of information being omitted from a blueprint or set of specifications.

- *Workman's compensation insurance*   Covers your homebuilder if someone working on your new home is injured.

- *Flood and earthquake (where applicable)*   Covers your homebuilder's costs of rebuilding your new home in the event of a flood or earthquake.

The three most important insurances to you are general liability, builder's risk, and workman's compensation (workman's comp).

The cost of these insurances varies depending on the type of construction your builder engages in, the volume of business he has, and, as with most insurance, his past claims record. A small custom homebuilder building only a dozen or so homes per year can expect to pay more than $50,000 per year for general liability insurance, and workman's comp can exceed 150% of payroll costs.

Don't let me scare you. If you build your own house, these costs are much lower but still substantial. But even if you aren't the general contractor, I strongly advise you to contact your current homeowner's insurance company to be sure you have adequate coverage during the course of construction. Often, you can get a rider on your existing homeowner's policy for any additional coverage you need for a nominal cost. I can't be more specific here because of all the variables involved in your construction project. Contact your homeowner's insurance company for more details. Don't forget to shop around. Do your "home" work and remember to negotiate.

Why You Should Contact the Homebuilder's Insurance Company

When you're about to make a decision on hiring a homebuilder, be sure to ask for a copy of his insurance certificates, general liability, builder's risk, and workman's comp. This next suggestion is not to protect you from the 99.9% of the good contractors out there; it's for the remaining 0.1% who aren't good. Don't just ask for copies of the certificates; have the homebuilder give you the names of the insurance companies and telephone numbers of the agents. Contact the insurance companies, and ask that they fax a copy of your homebuilder's insurance certificates directly to you. Remember, the kind of homebuilder who tells you he has insurance when he doesn't will also give you false documents. A homebuilder who has actually paid all that money to be insured properly will be happy to share the good news with you.

An easy way to be sure your homebuilder's insurance doesn't lapse is to request that he add you to his insurance policy as an "additional insured." This way, if your homebuilder does allow his insurance to lapse, the insurance company notifies all people listed as an additional insured of the lapse automatically. The builder should notify the insurance company and request that the certificate or proof of insurance be sent directly to you. What's important for you to know is that you should never accept any kind of insurance certificate from anyone except from the company providing the insurance.

To be added as an additional insured to someone's insurance policy, generally there's a charge that you or the homebuilder need to pay. The charge is usually about $50. This simple step and $50 can give you protection and peace of mind.

Summary

This chapter has discussed how much and how many different insurances your homebuilder carries. You learned the importance of the different types of insurance you need to build your own house and that if you paid for all these insurances, you could no longer afford to build your house. Knowing all that, be sure your homebuilder has the proper insurance he needs to protect you. When you find a good builder, it's worth not having to pay for the necessary insurances or assume all the liability of building a home.

How to Apply Yourself to Getting a Construction Loan

The loan application and prequalifying is the first and most important step in the entire process of building your home. You can't begin a conversation with your realtor and you can't discuss any plans with your builder until you have been prequalified.

Prequalifying is simply being approved for your new home loan. It's not all that simple, but it's important. The amount you are prequalified for is the total amount you can spend on your new home.

3

In this chapter:

* Learn the importance of being pre-qualified by your lender

* See how your builder goes from "dollars on the dirt" to your new home

* Find out how to best prepare for your loan application

* Get your credit report and discover how easy it is to clean it up

* Understand your FICO score and how it affects the amount of money you can borrow and the interest rate you have to pay

* See how amortization works by following an example

* To find out how to download a free sample loan application, see page 4

To do list

- ☐ Find a good lender.
- ☐ Choose the right loan package.
- ☐ Get prequalified for your loan to know your "dollars on the dirt."
- ☐ Find the land you want and what it will cost you.
- ☐ Speak with several builders to understand what you can get for your money.

Knowing Your "Dollars on the Dirt" Before You Begin

The prequalified amount is important because it's the amount of home you can buy. When you meet with your realtor for the first time—that is, if you have one—the first question he or she asks is "How much are you prequalified for?" If you don't know, you have to go away, find out, and come back when you do. (For more on whether you need a realtor, see the Caution in this section.)

The total amount you can spend includes equity in the home you might be selling. That *equity* (the difference between what you currently owe and what your home can sell for, minus real estate commissions and other expenses) combined with the amount you can borrow determine the total budget for your new home, including the land. If you already own the land, that prequalified amount can then be applied solely to the house. If you don't already own land and you're looking for a good piece of undeveloped property, the following are the kinds of questions a realtor would ask you to determine what you're looking for. These are questions you should answer regardless of whether you actually have a realtor:

- Where do you want the lot to be located?
- What school district do you want to live in?
- How long a commute to work do you want?
- How much acreage and how many square feet of house do you need?
- What kind of view do you want?
- Do you want to live in a gated community?
- Do you want flat terrain?
- Have you chosen a builder? Does he include the land in his transaction, or will it be separate?
- If the land is separate, how much do you have to spend on the land and how much will go toward building your new home?

After you have answered all these questions and determined the type, location, and amount you want to spend on the land, you can then begin looking for your property.

Assume you have been prequalified, found your realtor (if applicable), and found and purchased your land. Now you're ready to discuss building your new home. When you meet with your builder, all he wants to know is how much you have to spend on your new home.

His question might sound like the old car-salesperson conversation: You ask, "How much will this car cost me each month?" and he replies, "How much can you afford?"

note If you're buying a tract home, the land is almost always included. When purchasing a custom or semi-custom home, often the land costs extra and might not be included. Many times, people buy the land first, and then find a builder to build on it. You need to make all these decisions before you begin your homebuilding process.

How the Builder Goes from "Dollars on the Dirt" to Your New Home

The amount you have to spend is the most important answer you can give the builder during your conversation because it tells him how many "dollars on the dirt" you have. Here's how it works:

The builder usually asks a follow-up question, such as what kind of kitchen countertops you're looking for: Formica, Corian, solid surface, tile, or granite. The answer to this question tells the builder what your tastes are. For example, if you tell him the countertops have to be granite, he knows the bathroom needs to be tile, the lighting and plumbing fixtures need to be upgraded, and more floor tile than carpet is needed. If you answer that Formica is fine, he knows that cultured marble, standard lighting and plumbing fixtures, and carpet throughout are probably fine.

caution Remember, you don't always need a realtor to acquire your property. In many cases, your homebuilder sells you the land as part of the process of building your new home. If you already have a realtor representing you in the construction of your new home, your homebuilder is obligated to pay a commission, which usually gets added to the cost of your new home. Many, if not most, homebuilders (except for production home builders) don't build realtor commissions into their square footage costs. Sometimes a realtor does no more than contact your homebuilder yet can claim a full commission, which you pay.

This single answer indicates to your builder a narrow price range per square foot he can build your new home for while meeting your expectations. Standard selects, such as Formica or solid surface, might bring the construction cost down to $80 to $90 per square foot, but the granite answer might raise the construction

note See Chapter 10, "Selects and the 5,000 Decisions You Need to Make," for more information on standard selects.

cost to $150 to $160 per square foot or more. Of course, there's more to figuring the price per square foot than that, but knowing the type of countertops you prefer is a great starting point for estimating a range of construction costs for your new home.

Okay, now that the builder knows how much you have to spend and your taste in kitchen countertops, he looks at your lot size and then says, "Your new home will have a southern exposure and a three-car garage with metal garage doors. The exterior will be stucco with architectural features and a tile roof. The home will be a two-story, 2,800-square-foot Mission style, with solid surface countertops, tile floors in the kitchen and bath, carpet throughout the rest of the home, and mid-range lighting and plumbing fixtures. You'll have 2×6-foot exterior wall construction, with R-19 blown-in foam insulation, an R-32 ceiling, oak cabinetry and stair rails, double-hung and double-pane insulated windows, two fireplaces, and a designer front door." Then you say "What? How'd you do that?"

The builder knows what most people are looking for in their new homes. He knows what he can include in his cost of construction, such as carpet, lighting, plumbing, fireplaces, and front door. He knows how much you have to spend, so he simply divides that number by his cost per square foot and then knows the maximum number of square feet he can build. He can see by the shape and size of your lot that to get that number of square feet, you have to go up to a second story. He can get all this information from learning how much you have to spend and what kind of countertops you like.

At this point, most of your questions and design elements have been established, at least to begin with. From here, everything is an upgrade or an add-on. It all gets down to dollars on the dirt.

So now you need to determine your own dollars on your dirt. Before you begin this process, however, you need to go through a few steps, discussed in the following sections.

Finding a Lender

The first step is to find a lender. Lenders can come in many forms. You might want to go back to the lender for the house you're living in now. If you don't have a current lender, you might want to go to the bank where you have your checking account and credit cards.

If neither situation applies, you need to find a lender yourself, which can be a bank, a credit

> **tip**
> Many builders have their own lenders and can get you a better deal if you use them (or a penalty if you don't). Find out ahead of time. Some builders might even throw in a swimming pool or other perk if you use their lenders.

union, or a mortgage broker. All are good choices, but you need to speak with a few and find out the details. Here's where it gets complicated.

Choosing the Right Loan Package

I don't have the space in this book to discuss all the possible types of loans. There are VA loans; Fannie Mae; reverse mortgages for seniors; Housing and Urban Development's (HUD's) home equity conversion mortgage (HECM); 15-, 20-, and 30-year fixed rate; adjustable rate mortgage (ARM); interest first; no principal (also called interest only); balloon payment; employer assisted; energy efficient; pledge assist; and more. Don't get scared. When you sit down with your lender of choice, he asks you a few questions, much as the builder does, and narrows down your choices to one or two possibilities that are right for you.

At this point, you need to understand what lenders are offering, take notes, and then shop around for the best deal. There are a lot of variables, so comparing apples to apples is important. If you already have a trusted lender, usually he presents the best deal he has available to keep you as his customer. Even though it's the best deal that lender has, however, it might not be the best deal you can find. Check around. Look on the Internet to learn more about mortgage types and rates. Websites such as PickMyMortgage (http://www.pickmymortgage.com) can help you go through the steps of understanding the process.

Getting Prequalified

When you have chosen a lender and a type of loan that's right for you, you know approximately how many dollars on the dirt you have and what your expected monthly payment will be. Keep in mind these figures are estimates and don't include taxes, insurance, and homeowner's association (HOA) fees. The accurate amount can't be calculated until you do the following:

1. Determine the actual amount of yearly taxes, insurances, and HOA fees.
2. Lock in an interest rate.
3. Determine your down payment.
4. Estimate the remaining equity in your current home after the sale, closing costs, and realtor fees.
5. The lender evaluates your credit report, income-to-debt ratio, and payment history.

Again, gathering this information seems like a lot to do, but professionals calculate it one step at a time.

It seems complicated, but when you and your lender/realtor/homebuilder put a pen to paper and add up the figures, you can quickly determine how much is left over for the house portion of your project.

To get prequalified, first you're asked to fill out a loan app (application). The lender helps you with this document and makes it as painless as possible. He or she asks you a lot of questions about your financial background and current financial condition and asks you to sign a release allowing the lender to run a credit report. (See "Running Your Own Credit Report" later in this chapter for more information.)

To do list

- ☐ Record the account numbers for all your credit cards.
- ☐ Record the numbers for all your checking, saving, and credit union accounts.
- ☐ Gather information on your address and work history.
- ☐ Gather up your last two federal income tax statements, your last two paycheck stubs, and the other documents listed in the last part of this section.

Accumulating All Your Financial Records

In most cases, especially if you don't have any history with your lender, you need to accumulate two years of financial records. These records, coupled with your current credit report, tell the lender your average income over the past two years and verify that you have worked at the same location for that long. This information tells the lender that there's a good chance you'll continue working there and have reasonable expectations of promotions, raises, or at least cost of living adjustments (COLAs). All this information says that your income will, most likely, be stable.

note Accumulating all your financial records also includes the financial records of your spouse or legal significant other, if applicable. When assessing your loan amount, your lender takes into account the combined legal incomes and debts.

Listing Your Credit Card Accounts

Having your credit card numbers handy simply helps with the process of completing the loan app. Your credit card accounts show up on your credit report, but having them available when you're filling out your loan app is helpful.

Recording Your Other Account Numbers

It's also helpful to bring your account numbers for checking, savings, and credit union accounts. Be sure to remember all accounts you have had within the past two years. Don't try to hide anything. The lender you have selected wants to work with you, and he wants his commission on the loan. Any loan officer you authorize to process your loan has access to all your personal financial information, so be honest and let your lender work through any issues you might have.

Gathering Your Address and Work History

During the course of the loan app process, you're asked to provide your current address and any other addresses you've had over the past five years. This information gives the lender an idea of your stability.

As I mentioned previously, you also need to provide information about your spouse (if any) and your employer. You and your spouse need to bring your two most recent pay stubs. Again, this information verifies the amount of your combined income and that you and your spouse are actually employed.

Other Documentation

You also need to bring copies of your federal income tax statements for the past two years, which verifies your income and helps establish what's called your *income-to-debt ratio*—that is, how much you're earning and how much you're spending. This ratio helps determine how much you can pay each month in a combined mortgage payment (principal, interest, taxes, insurance, and HOA fees).

Before you go to your lender, you should be sure you have all the following documents to help speed your loan process:

- Your past two years of federal income tax statements

- Your last two pay stubs for both you and your spouse with company name and contact information

- Your monthly HOA statement

- Your last property tax statement

- Existing mortgage statements (first and second if applicable)

- Other debt statements

- Your additional income statements, such as child support, trust fund, investment income, dividends, interest, and rental income

caution Self-employment sends up a red flag to a potential lender but can be worked through. Even unemployment can be worked around. Your new loan amount and interest rate are based on two things: your debt-to-income ratio and past payment history. Both your current debt and your past payment history are a matter of record. Your income is what you claim it to be, but a W-2 makes it easy to verify. If you're self-employed, you create the W2s (if you draw a salary from your own company) and answer the Verification of Employment form the lender uses for verification of income. See the problem?

Many lenders accept the past two years of filed federal income tax statements, or they might suggest a "no-doc" loan that doesn't need income verification. This loan can be used only if your FICO (Fair Isaac Corporation; see "Understanding Your FICO Score" later in this chapter) score is high and the "loan to value" on the home is low, which create a low-risk situation for the lender.

tip Credit card debt is the killer. If you can, you might want to let your lender know that certain credit cards, car loans, or other debts will be paid out of the proceeds from the sale of existing home. This way, the amount of monthly bills is reduced, giving you more of your income to pay the new mortgage.

- All your bank account numbers, including checking, savings, money markets, and so forth
- Any other debt or income account numbers

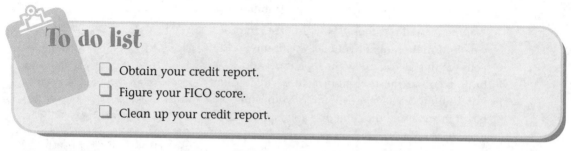

To do list

- ☐ Obtain your credit report.
- ☐ Figure your FICO score.
- ☐ Clean up your credit report.

Running Your Own Credit Report

Definition

The infamous credit report. Credit-reporting agencies maintain files on millions of borrowers, including you and me. Lenders making credit decisions buy credit reports on their prospects, applicants, and customers from credit-reporting agencies. Your *credit report* details your credit history as it has been reported to the credit-reporting agency by lenders who have extended credit to you. Your credit report lists what types of credit you use, the length of time your accounts have been open, and whether you've paid your bills on time. It tells lenders how much credit you've used and whether you're seeking new sources of credit. These reports give lenders a broader view of your credit history than do other data sources, such as a bank's own customer data.

Your credit report reveals many aspects of your borrowing activities. All pieces of information should be considered in relationship to other pieces of information. Credit scoring is useful because it makes it possible to consider all this information quickly, fairly, and consistently.

Where to Find Your Credit Reports

Under the Consumer Reporting Act, you're entitled to a copy of all the information a credit bureau has on you. You need to find out what credit bureaus are telling people about you and find out who has been asking. Credit bureaus are *not* consumer friendly. They exist to protect businesses and banks from consumers. To do this, they calculate a credit score. This score is based on all the information in your credit report: history, late payments, paying ahead, amount of credit, over what period of time, and so forth.

The most common credit score is the FICO score, and lenders base their approval on this score. You have three FICO scores, one for each credit bureau, and you can get all three scores from myFICO (http://www.myfico.com). For more information, go to the myFICO site, or contact each credit bureau individually:

- *Equifax*   800-685-1111, http://www.equifax.com
- *Experian (formerly TRW)*   888-397-3742, http://www.experian.com
- *TransUnion*   800-888-4213, http://www.transunion.com

Understanding Your FICO Score

Credit bureau scores are often called "FICO scores" because most credit bureau scores used in the United States and Canada are produced from software developed by Fair Isaac Corporation (FICO). The three major credit-reporting agencies—Equifax, Experian, and TransUnion—provide FICO scores to lenders.

FICO scores give lenders the best guide to future consumer risk, based solely on credit report data. The higher the score, the lower the risk. No score says whether a specific person will be a "good" or "bad" customer, however. And although many lenders use FICO scores to help them make lending decisions, each lender has its own strategy, including the level of risk it finds acceptable for a given credit product. There's no single "cutoff score" used by all lenders. The major score categories are below 620, 620 to 690, 690 to 740, 740 to 780, and above 780, with each category containing about 20% of the total overall U.S. population. The average score that's also considered a good score is 690 to 740.

Depending on your FICO score, you're loaned what is called "hard" or "soft" money. You get *hard money* when your credit is bad and your interest rate is high, and *soft money* when your credit is good and you can secure a lower interest rate. Table 3.1 shows the difference between hard and soft money.

How Your FICO Score Relates to Your Loan

Your FICO Score	Your Interest Rate	Your Monthly Payment
720–850	5.56%	$858
700–719	5.69%	$869
675–699	6.23%	$921
620–674	7.38%	$1,036
560–619	8.53%	$1,157
500–559	9.29%	$1,238

As you can see by this table, a difference of 161 points on your FICO score can mean the difference between 5.56% and 9.29% annual percentage rate (APR), or an increase in your monthly payment by $380 per month. If you paid this higher rate over the life of a 30-year loan, it would cost you $136,800—certainly reason enough to clean up your credit report.

How to Clean Up Your Credit Report

Now that you know about credit reports, how's your credit rating? Is your credit report accurate? Probably not. You need to check your credit report once a year or at least before you go to a lender to get prequalified for a loan, whether it's for a home, car, boat, whatever. Your credit report affects your interest rate and your monthly loan payment.

Credit reports can contain errors, often because the report is incomplete or contains information about someone else. Typically, these errors happen because you applied for credit under different names (using both Robert Jones and Bob Jones, for example), someone made a clerical error in reading or entering a name or address from a handwritten application, your social security number is wrong because of a typo or the lender misread the number, or loan or credit card payments were inadvertently applied to the wrong account.

A good credit score is important to you during the prequalification process because a better score gets you better interest rates. Better interest rates lower the amount of money you have to pay back and lower your monthly payment. This decrease can mean hundreds of dollars less you pay each month or hundreds more square feet in your new house.

I don't want to scare you with all this intimidating information without giving you at least a small ray of sunshine. Forget all the horror stories you've heard about cleaning up your credit report. A miracle has happened: Even though credit bureaus have traditionally been unfriendly to consumers because their primary responsibility is to protect their clients (businesses and banks) from consumers, recently it's become easier for you to generate a credit report and correct any mistakes in it.

caution You also need to check your credit report once a year because it helps prevent identity theft. With information readily available on the Internet and personal data being traded, sold, and stolen every day, a credit report is the fastest way to discover whether someone is using your identity to get credit. Identity theft is a real problem, and you don't want to find out yours has been stolen at the exact time you're ready to begin building your new home and need that loan. The sooner you catch it, the less difficult and time consuming it is to correct. The good news is that because identity theft does happen so often, banks, credit card companies, and other financial institutions have systems in place to help you, and in most cases, they assume all the charges your identity thief has racked up.

To see how easy it is now to get your credit report and correct any mistakes, choose one of the three credit bureaus' websites listed previously. Create an account by answering all the questions asked at the site. There will be a lot of prying questions, so keep your cool and be patient. When you have succeeded, you'll actually see (and be able to print) your up-to-date credit report! It really is that easy.

If your report has any negative entries, they are listed at the top. Here's the good part: Next to each entry is a Dispute button. Click the button for the first item to be disputed and fill in a paragraph or two explaining why you don't think it should be there. Click the Submit button, and then go to the next entry. When you're finished, you see a message saying that you'll be notified within 30 days with an updated credit report.

When doing the research for this book, this is exactly what I did, and in 30 days, I was notified. I clicked the Get Report link, and four of the five items I disputed were gone. It's that easy!

The five negative items on the credit report were all health insurance related: a few lab invoices and a doctor's office visit. In the dispute response section of the initial report, I provided my health insurance carrier, group number, and an explanation of why the bill should have been already paid. This information was sent to the credit collection company that reported me to the original provider. The company reporting the collections has 30 days to respond when you dispute an entry. If the collection agency doesn't respond *or* agrees with your explanation, the item is dropped. If the collection agency disagrees, the credit bureau sends you contact information so that you can try to resolve the collection yourself. In my case, the four lab invoices were dropped. For the remaining item, the doctor's office visit, all I needed to do was call to work it out.

The credit bureau you use is supposed to notify the other two bureaus to remove the successfully disputed entries, but as they are competitors, this notification doesn't always happen. It's your responsibility to follow the same procedure with the two remaining bureaus.

Amortization Made Simple

Are you familiar with the *Rule of 72s*? That's what the financial industry calls the formula used to calculate how much you owe on your loan each month for the life of your loan. It's a complicated formula, as each month you pay down a certain amount of principal and a certain amount of interest, so for the following month, the remaining loan amount is different. Each month, the amount of principal owed and the amount of time the balance will be outstanding change, which affects the amount of remaining interest, which affects the amount of principal that can be paid in that one payment, considering that the monthly payment has to stay the same every month for the life of the loan. Also figured into this equation is that the lender wants a much larger share of his interest paid to him before you ever get around to applying the payment to what you owe.

Work Through an Amortization Example

Here's an example of the Rule of 72s:

1. You borrow $250,000 at 6.5% APR for 30 years in a standard mortgage.

2. Your monthly mortgage payment (principal and interest) calculates as $1,580.17. If you made your payment every month for the life of the loan and paid the loan off, here's what you would have paid back:

   - *Total principal paid* $250,000.00
   - *Total interest paid* $318,861.20
   - *Total repaid (principal plus interest)* $568,861.20
   - *The actual interest percentage on the principal*   127.544%

Wait, you borrow $250,000 and you have to pay back more than a half a million dollars. Sound like something from gangster movie? No, it's just the Rule of 72s, and it's legal. Really.

Now, I know you think it couldn't get any worse than that, but here goes: The Rule of 72s is designed so that the lender gets most of his interest paid back up front. So if you pay off the loan before the 30 years are up or even in the first few years, the lender gets nearly all his interest on the loan, and you still owe the majority of what you borrowed. That's what is called *amortization*.

In the United States today, the average homeowner sells his or her home every seven years. That means the average 30-year mortgage is paid off early, every seven years after payment #84 and a new mortgage is started. Using the same scenario, at the end of seven years when you ask your lender for a payoff, you'll be told that by making monthly payments of $1,580.17 each month for seven years, you have paid in $132,734.97.

What do you still owe on the $250,000? $226,040.65! That's right. You've paid down only $23,959.35 in seven years after paying a total of $132,734.28. Of that total, $108,774.93 went to pay back the lender's interest, and only $23,959.35 went toward the $250,000 you borrowed.

Take a look at this: The first mortgage payment you make breaks down like this:

- *Total payment* $1,580.17
- *Interest* $1,354.17
- *Principal* $226.00

Does that breakdown make you want to break down? Don't get upset about it. Everyone who owns a mortgage has the same deal. Most just don't know it or don't want to.

Today, fewer people actually want to pay off a 30-year conventional loan. The average U.S. homeowner today buys and sells his or her home every seven years. As a result, there's a huge trend today toward *interest-only* loans. With these loans, you pay only the interest and none of the principal. This arrangement keeps your monthly mortgage payment as low as possible, increasing the amount you can afford each month. Most people figure that the incredible appreciation real estate has been realizing over the past few years will more than compensate for the interest paid, and 100% of the loan payments are tax deductible.

Summary

In this chapter, you learned the importance of being prequalified by your lender. You also learned how your builder goes from "dollars on the dirt" to your new home—starting with your budget, he can tell you how many square feet, the number of floors, the type of countertops, the number of bathrooms, what kind of kitchen, and so forth your money will buy.

You also learned how to best prepare for your loan application and saw how easy it is to get your credit report and have it cleaned up.

Finally, I tried to give you a better understanding of your FICO score and how it affects the amount of money you can borrow and the interest rate you have to pay. You also stepped through an example of how amortization works. Did that take you by surprise? It sure took me by surprise the first time I learned how it worked.

See "Additional Resources" on page 4 for details on how to download a free sample loan application.

A Few Key Clauses to Consider in Your Contracts

4

This is a book about buying, building, and renovating your new home. I don't have the space here and you don't have the time for me to go into contracts or contract law in depth. I do, however, want to discuss a few ideas that might help you with your contracts.

You need to be aware of two truths when it comes to agreements and contracts:

- The only time they have any value is when something goes wrong.
- They are only as good as the amount of money and time you have to throw at them.

To do list

- ☐ If you think there's a problem with the construction of your home, first contact your builder, discuss the issue with him, and find out what he has to say about it.

- ☐ Talk to your homebuilder directly, but also fax him to have a written record of your communication with him.

- ☐ If your builder is unresponsive or you are otherwise still unsatisfied, contact your state's Registrar of Contractors Office (or your state's equivalent).

- ☐ Contact your attorney as a last resort if your problem still hasn't been remedied.

What's the Value of a Good Agreement?

The simple explanation of an *agreement*, or contract, is that it establishes "I'll do this, if you'll do that"—it describes both parties' obligations. It contains the time frame, or *term*, in which each party agrees to do "this" and "that" and how to resolve the situation if one of the parties doesn't do "this" or won't do "that," which is called the *remedy*. If both parties fulfill their obligations as called for in their contract, they never have to look at that agreement or contract again. That's the goal.

If the person you have contracted with, such as your homebuilder, doesn't perform the tasks he's agreed to do, you and your attorney pull out the agreement and see what the next steps are in remedying the situation. For building a new home, the agreement is fairly straightforward. The builder agrees to build you a new home, in the manner you want it built, in a legal fashion, and in a timely manner. You agree to provide necessary information for constructing that new home in a timely manner and further agree to pay the builder based on completed milestones (or draws).

note For more information on draws, see Chapter 15, "The Importance of Your Financial Draws."

If you run into a problem or believe that your homebuilder isn't living up to his part of the agreement, you must first communicate with your builder. Remember, you should almost never have a problem that requires you and your attorney to look at your contracts again. Don't get alarmed at the first sign of trouble and call your attorney. If you have a problem, call your builder. Speak with him to find out what's going on. Have him explain the reason for the situation.

In almost every case, it's only a misunderstanding and can be resolved easily. The key is communication. Call your homebuilder and, most important, fax him. This way, he's sure to see your question or concern, and in case it isn't resolved easily, you both have a paper trail or written record.

DON'T PANIC–ALWAYS CALL YOUR BUILDER IF YOU HAVE A CONCERN

Often homeowners are unhappy because they simply don't understand the building process, which this book should solve. The most common cause of misunderstandings happens when your homebuilder is waiting for a government inspection or is scheduling the next subcontractor.

Homeowners always get upset when they see nothing happening with their home for several days. They start thinking, "The horror stories are true! The homebuilder took off with all my money!" or "Why has he forgotten about *my* house? What's he thinking? I'll show him!"

Most likely, the homebuilder is waiting on the strapping and shear inspection from the county or, even though it stopped raining three days ago, is waiting for the stucco to dry completely before applying the final topcoat. Call your builder before you get upset.

Unfortunately, there might come a time when you have placed several calls to your builder that remain unanswered, he does something you asked him not to do, he builds something incorrectly and refuses to fix it, or whatever. If this happens, the first thing to do is contact your state's Registrar of Contractors Office (or your state's equivalent). For more information on contacting this office, see "Check Business Licensing and Trade Associations" in Chapter 6, "Doing Your 'Home' Work on Your Homebuilder."

If all else fails, call your attorney, but don't move on to this step until you have exhausted all other measures. Calling your attorney leads to your builder being served with a summons, which is an open declaration of war. If your builder gets served, all work on your house stops at that point. Your home project will shut down cold until the situation gets resolved.

In my experience, when you have your attorney serve your builder, it costs approximately $5,000 for your attorney's retainer fee and most likely another $5,000 in legal fees to see it through to conclusion. So before you flip this switch, be sure you want to shut down your project and shell out another $10,000 to get your builder's attention.

The other serious problem is that with the current backlog of civil cases, you could be looking at as much as 24 months until you go before a judge if the case goes to trial. That means $10,000 and up to two years of your project remaining dormant. This is worse than just the time and money; it's two years of stress and two years you have to live elsewhere in the meantime. Are you in an apartment? Are you selling the home you're currently living in? You really don't want to have to find a place to live for the next two years.

Time, money, stress, and inconvenience are good reasons to make another effort to communicate with your builder. It's always in both your best interests to resolve any issues you have before you get to legal action. You both want to build the house you want, and by keeping a calm head and maintaining communication, almost anything can be worked out. Use the legal system only as a last resort.

Who Is the American Arbitration Association?

This AAA isn't about automobiles. It's about binding arbitration. The American Arbitration Association (AAA; http://www.adr.org) is there to help you through legal resolutions.

The AAA is a not-for-profit, public service organization committed to resolving disputes through the use of arbitration, mediation, and other voluntary procedures. The reason for its authority is that both parties—in this case, you and your homebuilder—at the time of signing (execution) agreed they would play by the AAA rules if a dispute arose.

The AAA was developed to provide a low-cost, streamlined process to resolve disputes between consumers and businesses whose contracts contain a standardized arbitration clause. With this clause, terms and conditions are non-negotiable in most or all of a contract's terms, conditions, features, and choices. That means your agreements and contracts must include an AAA binding arbitration clause. Be sure it's added to any agreement you sign. It's as simple as copying and pasting a paragraph the AAA supplies. (See "A Sample Binding Arbitration Clause" later in this chapter.)

In short, binding arbitration replaces the court system with an efficient, cost-effective, and expedient way of resolving legal disputes between you and your homebuilder. *Arbitration* refers to having both sides of the argument heard by a qualified, impartial, legal mediator, and *binding* means that the results are legally binding or final—they can't be appealed or overturned.

note In 2002, more than 230,000 cases were filed with the AAA in a range of areas, including finance, construction, labor and employment, insurance, and technology. The AAA has 36 offices in the United States and Europe.

As an administrative agency, the AAA processes a case from filing to closing, appointing arbitrators, setting hearings, transmitting documents, and scheduling conference calls. The goal is to keep cases moving in a fair and impartial process until completion. In many cases, the AAA responds to a claim the same week you file it. Based on my experience, AAA procedures are scheduled, performed, and concluded in under 30 days.

Definition

The arbitration process is similar to what takes place in a court but is much less formal. An independent neutral person hears the evidence and issues a decision, which is known as an *award*. This award is generally final and binding on the parties in the case. The key is "final and binding." That means neither party can take the decision to a higher court to have it overturned, burn more legal hours, and harass one another with legal expenses or stall tactics. The only time you or your builder can insist on taking legal action with a civil court or small claims court is if the amount of money you or your builder is seeking falls within the limits set for small claims courts in the state in which you or your builder lives or operates.

Arbitrators are independent contractors who hear the evidence and decide the outcomes of cases. Although they are not employees of the AAA, arbitrators (often referred to as *neutrals*) are carefully selected for their expertise and trained extensively by the AAA. In consumer cases, the AAA appoints an arbitrator who is an attorney or an actual judge, unless the parties agree otherwise. For example, in a case with many financial records, the parties might agree to use an arbitrator who is an accountant instead of an attorney or judge.

To file a claim with the AAA, you can contact its Case Management Centers in Atlanta, Dallas, Fresno, and East Providence. You can find address information on the AAA's website. In-person hearings, if any are needed, can be held at any location convenient to both you and your homebuilder.

note The American Arbitration Association also provides *mediation* and *binding mediation* services. These services can be used to resolve issues and misunderstanding between you and the homebuilder. The primary difference between mediation and arbitration is in mediation, the AAA provides a mediator and attempts to discuss and agree to a resolution. In arbitration, the AAA provides someone who listens to both sides and renders a judgment or decision as to the resolution or outcome. The terms *binding* and *nonbinding* have the same definition when applied to mediation and arbitration. The outcome of nonbinding decisions can be appealed or argued in court, whereas the outcome of binding decisions can't be.

Definition

tip One of the many benefits of arbitration is that an attorney can represent either party. Although having an attorney participate in your arbitration proceeding isn't required, I do recommend you have one present because he or she can present a better case (without any emotion you might have) and be able to cite legal precedents you're probably not familiar with. An attorney adds to the overall cost but increases your likelihood of a favorable outcome.

To begin the process, either you or your homebuilder can use the Demand for Arbitration form in the Forms drop-down list on the AAA's website (http://www.adr.org). Send the completed form, along with a copy of the arbitration provision in your contract and the appropriate filing fees and deposits to any AAA office. The AAA then notifies your builder, advising him that the AAA has received a consumer case.

If your claim for actual damages does not exceed $10,000, your cost is set at $125. If your claim is between $10,000 and $75,000, your cost is set at $375. The homebuilder is responsible for all other arbitration costs in these cases. Most homebuyer-homebuilder disputes fall into this category of $75,000 or less. That means your cost is usually between $125 and $375 for court costs, with no attorneys! If your claim for actual damages exceeds $75,000, you're responsible for costs as set forth in the Commercial Dispute Resolution Procedures Fee Schedule, which is listed on the AAA website.

Additionally, many disputes can be resolved simply by reviewing the documents; however, either party can request a hearing. This request should be made no later than 10 days after the AAA has initiated the case. You can request a telephone hearing or an in-person hearing.

If your builder refuses to participate after being properly notified of the arbitration proceeding, the arbitrator can make a decision based on the documents you provide as evidence. This means you might win simply by default.

> **note** The American Arbitration Association and the use of arbitration are specifically designed to eliminate attorneys, courts, and associated fees and lengthy processes. The intent is to make the process inexpensive and quick. Whereas the AAA states that no attorneys are necessary, this doesn't prevent you or your homebuilder from being represented by one. If either party opts for an attorney, you can be assured the process will cost considerably more for both parties and take much longer. Although my experience has shown that both parties respect the intent of arbitration, some do not. Some homebuilders don't agree to arbitration, with the intent to deliberately expose the homebuyer to the expensive court/attorney process to deter potential confrontation from the homebuyer.

For more specific information on the rules and fees for construction-related filings, visit http://www.adr.org/sp.asp?id=22004.

Don't forget: Either the homebuyer or the homebuilder can start an arbitration proceeding. This means both you and your builder have to follow the obligations of your agreements or contracts.

> **note** Although the AAA is the most recognized and respected arbitration organization in the United States today, other organizations can provide these services.

A Sample Binding Arbitration Clause

Here's a typical sample of what a binding arbitration clause should look like. To provide for binding arbitration of any disputes arising from any contract, all you have to do is insert the following clause into your contract or agreement:

> "Any controversy or claim arising out of or relating to this contract, or the breach thereof, shall be settled by arbitration administered by the American Arbitration Association in accordance with its Commercial Arbitration Rules and judgment on the award rendered by the arbitrator(s) may be entered in any court having jurisdiction thereof."

You can find this wording at www.adr.org/sp.asp?id=22297.

caution This book does not attempt to provide legal counsel, written or implied, in any way whatsoever. You must consult your own legal counsel for the proper advice on your unique circumstances, the laws in your state, and local jurisdiction.

To do list

- ☐ Discuss all soft costs with your homebuilder before you sign any contracts.
- ☐ Determine whether the homebuilder expects you to pay for any of these costs.
- ☐ Make it clear to the homebuilder that he should pay for all soft costs unless he can justify you handling the expense.
- ☐ Ensure that you come to an agreement on how to handle all soft costs before you sign any contracts.

What Are Soft Costs, and Why Are They in Contracts?

Soft costs need to be mentioned in the homebuyer-homebuilder contract. *Soft costs* are expenses that can be hidden (or just not mentioned) in agreements or specifications but billed to the homebuyer later as an extra. Typically, these costs are ones you might never think of, and they can add up if they're not specified at the start.

Soft costs can include fees for the following (which are just a few of the many possible, believe it or not): building permits, demolition permits, remediation (environmental cleanup), landfills, water meter purchase, filing and recording, plan check, plan and specification printing, delivery and postage, secretarial services, inspections, septic approval and inspection, delivery, electric meter installation, street addressing, soil and compaction testing, termite spraying, deposits, dust control, course of construction irrigation, trash removal, porta-potties, tree removal, and any outstanding fines.

Make Sure Soft Costs Are Included in the Fixed Costs of Your Contract

All these fees are customarily paid by the builder and are not the homeowner's responsibility. As the homeowner, you need to discuss any soft costs with your homebuilder and clarify whether any of the fees listed previously (or others) will be charged back to you, the homebuyer. Have your homebuilder justify any charges to you, and show him the following paragraph:

> CONTRACTOR: You are supposed to pay for the fees mentioned in this book, not charge them to this homebuyer. If there's any fee you think this homebuyer should pay, you need to explain it to the homebuyer and come to an agreement before you sign any contracts. Please hand this book back to your homebuyer now.

To do list

- ☐ Don't agree to any contract with a clause requiring you to make specs and selects within the first 30 days after signing the agreement.
- ☐ Agree to make all your specs and selects in a timely manner based on the building schedule the builder should provide for you.
- ☐ Make sure the building schedule includes critical path reminders to help you make all the selects you need at the appropriate points on the schedule.

Time Frame for Making Selects

Most builders have a clause in their contracts requiring homebuyers to make their specs and selects within the first 30 days after signing the agreement. Specs are the general building specifications included in the blueprint for your home. Selects are all the choices you make when picking out the design elements of your new home. (For more information on specs and selects, see Chapter 10, "Selects and the 5,000 Decisions You Need to Make.") Thirty days is not enough time to make all these decisions.

Make Your Selections Based on the Building Schedule

The reason homebuilders put the term at 30 days is because if they don't, most homebuyers let this period go on forever and create problems by not making decisions in time, which slows or halts the construction of your new home. So you, as the homebuyer, must take the responsibility to make all your specs and selects in a timely manner, but don't have an enforceable contract making you perform them too quickly. In the event of a different problem, homebuilders might use this clause to prove you are in breach of your agreement. They know that ahead of time because 30 days isn't reasonable.

Ask that the wording for this contract clause be something like this: "I agree to make all my specs and selects in a timely manner based on the building schedule the builder provides and with critical path reminders to me as needed."

Making every design decision that affects the entire house construction within the first 30 days is a daunting task at best. Speak with your homebuilder about setting up a selections-construction schedule. Most builders follow a schedule like this to keep your project on track. If you can follow his schedule, you have to make the appropriate decisions only when

> **note** *Critical path decision* is a project management term that means the decision is critical for keeping the project on schedule, and if the decision isn't made by a certain date, the project stops until it is.

called for at the time. If the agreement doesn't already have wording to this effect, ask your homebuilder to be sure that the verbiage in your agreement reflects you making your decisions as needed, not just in 30 days or at the signing of his agreement.

Summary

This chapter has discussed the value of an agreement and explained how to include a binding arbitration clause in all your agreements. You learned about circumventing the courts' long delays and high costs by submitting disputes to the American Arbitration Association for arbitration. Including an arbitration clause in *every* legal agreement you make, whether it's for building a house, hiring a professional, and so on, can save you a lot of time and money.

You also learned about including soft costs in contracts and changing the 30-day term for making specs and selects. Keep in mind that you and your builder can agree to making your selections based on your homebuilder's building schedule.

Building Your Team of Professionals

Building your team of professionals is an important step in building your new home. In addition to determining a good builder, you can realize great benefits from building relationships with a knowledgeable and professional realtor, title agent, and lender. They are the people who will assist you in building the best new home, in the best location, at the least expense, and for the lowest interest and be sure it's all done legally.

To do list

- [ ] Speak with your friends, family, and co-workers.
- [ ] Drive around the area you want to live in.
- [ ] Write down contact information of the realtors you see on signs.
- [ ] Call, meet, and interview these realtors.

Identifying the Best Realtor for You

The best way to find a realtor is through a personal reference. Ask your friends, your family, and your co-workers. Be prepared, however: When you choose a realtor this way, everyone you asked whose realtor you didn't choose will be a little ticked, but this decision is about you, not them.

Another way is to drive around your area. Look to see which realtors have the most signs up selling property. They're the ones with the most listings. They're popular, they know the area, and they're successful. Call them and put them on your list of potential candidates.

You have to pick a realtor who knows the area where you want to buy or build. Find realtors with experience in that specific area. They know the prices and know what's fair and reasonable and what's not. They know the comparable values (comps). They know the areas that will appreciate the most, which not only protects your investment, but also increases your investment equity. They know the school districts, shopping centers, future freeways, drug rehabilitation centers, homeowner's association (HOA) troubles, bankruptcies, repossessions, bargains, views, age of homes, good builders, and best values. All this knowledge is unique to a particular area. Outside realtors just don't know that level of detail.

caution Although builders certainly appreciate business from realtors, it's really not necessary to have a realtor as part of the construction process. Using a realtor can cost a substantial amount in commissions that you could otherwise put toward your home. Also, use caution when speaking with realtors, as they use various methods to "lock in" customers and commissions with the homebuilder. In many areas of the country, it has been necessary to create some rules and standards of conduct to address these ethical and professional issues with the real estate commissions. Your lender and builders can assist you with the house title and closing at the completion of your new home.

FINDING A REALTOR THROUGH REAL ESTATE COMPANIES

Another way to find the right realtor is to request information from real estate companies in the area. Ask for information on the company's total sales as well as the sales and listings of each realtor. Most realtors specialize in either listing homes for sale or actually selling homes. Each process requires different techniques, and realtors are usually better at one than the other. The real estate company can give you information on the number and dollar value of sales versus listings for each realtor. Also, many realtors focus on a certain price range of home. Some realtors specialize in production homes and others in high-end custom homes, for example. Interview the most successful realtors. They are successful for a reason. Be sure to inquire about their networks with corporations and professional associations, such as the medical association. If you're listing a house, I recommend requesting an advertising and promotional plan in writing.

Personally, I'm not as comfortable asking realtor companies to recommend themselves. I've collected data from real estate companies and didn't find it useful. It was often a bunch of hype. Personal recommendations have always worked best for me.

How to Locate a Good Realtor

You need to interview several realtors. Interview at least three, maybe more. Have them take you out for coffee or even lunch. Realtors are accustomed to buying clients lunch. During the interview, ask them the following questions:

- What is their experience?
- How long have they been selling?
- What did they do before that? (They all have done something before.)
- How many homes do they close on per year?
- How many listings do they have now?
- Have they sold new home construction?

I have to stop right here because that last question is crucial.

Most realtors aren't comfortable with new home construction sales. Most realtors, when a client asks for help buying a new custom home, push their clients into a production (tract) home. Buying this type of home is faster and easier, realtors know the market, and fewer things can go wrong, so their commissions are more secure. Remember, it's all about commission, and that's okay. Most people are all about the paycheck. If you don't want a production home, you need to specify that to your realtor. Ask right out, "Are you comfortable selling custom homes? How many custom homes have you sold? How many homebuilders have you worked with? Do you have a relationship with one or more now?"

If you don't hear the answers you were counting on, you need to explain to the realtor that you won't be working with him or her because you're looking for a realtor with new home sales experience and homebuilder relationships.

Determining Your Potential Realtor

Most realtors can quickly complete the one-page "previously owned home" sales contract, and the sales agent for the production home project can do new home contracts if the realtors convince you that a production home is the best way to go. Most realtors aren't comfortable with the eight-plus-page new home sales contract. Be sure to ask about their experience with new home sales, builders, and general contractors.

Get realtors to measure your home and estimate its comparable value (comp). Don't always go with the one who values your house the highest. It's like selling a car. If the car sells the first day, it's not because it was a great car. It's because you undervalued it and priced it too low. The same is true with your home. If it sells fast, it's not necessarily because the realtor is awesome; it's because you sold it too cheaply and you lost money. However, if a house is on the market for six months, it's overpriced.

Don't walk away from the realtor with the highest comps, however. My first house comped out at around $63,000. (Yes, this was more than 20 years ago.) I interviewed several realtors and one who came with a personal recommendation. He looked at my home and said, "I can get $120,000 for it." Yeah, right, that's twice as much, whatever. I wasn't in a hurry, so I signed a 30-day sales contract with him. Less than three weeks later, it sold for $120,000. That interview process alone made me close to $60,000 tax free! It happened again four years ago when I "shopped" realtors. All the comps came back at or near $360,000, and one realtor said, "I can get $400,000." He said, "I have to find only *one* buyer." Eighteen days later, SOLD! It was a decision worth $40,000. I'm up $100,000 just for taking my own advice. Of course, I can't promise you these same successes, but they really did happen to me.

These experiences are examples of realtors who are aggressive, professional, and self-confident. They understand that buying and selling a home is more an art than a science. They understand that comps are no more than a starting point. This is the type of real estate professional you want working for you when selling your existing home and, just as important, when locating and negotiating the purchase of your new home and property. They can help you negotiate the best price, structure the transaction to best protect you and your investment, and often save a transaction from falling through by coming up with creative solutions.

It's important to ask exactly what a realtor is going to do to market your home. This doesn't mean simply listing it on the multiple listing service (MLS). It also means the quality and quantity of flyers. Will they be color or just black and white? Will they be printed or just copied? What kinds of newspaper advertising will the realtor do? What open houses, cable TV advertising, and seller commission perks, incentives, and splits does the realtor plan to entice another agent to sell your home? Finally, be sure you feel comfortable with him or her. You don't have to be friends with your realtor, but you should feel as though you could be. If the chemistry isn't right, just find someone else.

caution Your realtor can also be helpful in timing when it's best to list your existing home for sale (if applicable). Remember, the average construction time of a new home is seven or more months and can take even longer. If you put your home on the market and it sells too quickly, you might have to move twice. If you place your home on the market too late, it could cause problems with converting your construction loan into a conventional mortgage because you would have to pay two mortgages each month until your existing home is sold. You could also sell your existing home with a seven-month future closing date, which can create difficulties for your potential buyers and might prohibit the sale of your home.

Your realtor can help you make these decisions and time the sale of your existing home to coincide with the completion of your new home.

To do list

- ☐ Introduce yourself to the residential loan officer in your own bank.
- ☐ Ask your realtor for introductions.
- ☐ Speak with friends, family, and co-workers.
- ☐ If you've chosen a homebuilder, ask him for a lender recommendation.

Getting Your Lender on Your Side

As I mentioned earlier, your lender relationship is an important one, too. The three nonconstruction relationships you'll have are with your lender, realtor, and title company. It's your lender who you'll communicate with the most. Your realtor is there in the beginning to help you purchase your land and at the end to close on your house. Your title company is there only at the end when you close. Your lender is there throughout the process, from getting you prequalified and securing your interest rate and loan to working with you and your homebuilder through the course of construction, monitoring the builder's progress, and administering and releasing funds. It's the lender who reviews all your personal financial information and determines how much you can borrow and what it will cost you.

A Lending Relationship Needs to Be Two-Way

For the reasons outlined in the previous section, the relationship you have with your lender is an important one. Find a lender you feel comfortable with. Interview several. Remember, lenders are selling products—money. All lenders sell their money for different prices and under different terms. I like to use mortgage brokers, who are just like insurance brokers. They broker, which means they represent many different products and lending institutions so that they can sell you the best and most cost-effective product.

A loan officer can sell only the loans his or her institution offers. A mortgage broker can shop around to find the best deal for you. The best deal depends on your credit score and other circumstances, such as the following:

- Being out of work or employed at your current employer for less than two years
- Having a bankruptcy on your credit report
- Having a bad credit score for some reason

Your lender or broker is on your side and will fight for you. Remember the discussion of a realtor's commission? To earn their commission, lenders and brokers want to do everything they can to get you funded the best way they can. As an example, on a $300,000 loan, a loan officer or mortgage broker makes about $1,200 personal commission.

Picking Your Lender

As with other professionals you hire, you need to feel comfortable with your lender, too. This professional is as important to you as your builder. Your lender can get you the most money and the lowest interest rate and help present your financial information in the best way possible. When you select a lender, you need to consider not only interest rates and closing costs, but also your ability to communicate with this person. *Communication.* I can't say this often enough, and when I don't say it, it's implied. Communicate with your lender, communicate with your realtor, communicate with your title company, and, most important, communicate with your builder. Force all your professionals who will be working for you to communicate. Notice I didn't say "with" you; when you're paying them, they work *for* you. It takes work to communicate, but it takes more work to undo problems and legal battles that can occur when you don't.

During the course of construction, the bank checks on your builder's progress and quality of work. No funds are released until you sign off on them. The money belongs to the bank until you approve giving it to the builder. At that point, the funds that go to the home-builder are owed by you, and you're now responsible for repaying them.

Walk the job site, and inspect your new home yourself. Verify that the home is being built to your specifications. Communicate with the builder any time you don't understand some-thing or if you think an error has been made. Ask a lot of questions. Communicate with your lender for the same reasons. If the builder has made an error or won't take the time to explain why something is being done, get his atten-tion. Call the lender and ask that he or she hold up the builder's next draw (payment). You'll be pleasantly surprised by how fast your builder calls you with the answer to whatever question you might have had. Communicate.

The remaining decisions for choosing a lender are technical: interest rate, loan amount, inter-est lock, points and other closing costs (such as appraisal of your existing home), filing fees, courier fees, and length of time to close the loan and begin construction.

Interview several potential lenders, ask their rates (all the technical information), and get a feel for how comfortable you'll be working with them.

> **caution** Some lenders have terms that your homebuilder is unable to adhere to or accept. For example, some lenders might require that a builder submit "no-lien agree-ments" from all subcontractors and service providers. Most builders, subcontractors, and service providers simply won't agree to that requirement. Introduce your homebuilder to your lender as early in the process as possi-ble, and encourage them to have these con-versations to be sure they can work together.

> **caution** Many produc-tion home-builders try to insist that you use their own lenders or mortgage companies. Remember how much the lender makes on the "paper" (loan). Builders can't force you to use their lenders. They can, however, entice you into using their lenders with incentives, such as a free $20,000 swimming pool. If their rates are fair and the incentives are good, do it (but you don't have to).

Who Selects the Title Company?

You, the homebuyer, by law get to pick the title company. I bought and sold my first six homes, and I didn't know that. I thought the realtor is the one who picks the title company. It's because the realtors always did, and I just let him. One reason the realtor usually picks the title insurance agent is that most people don't buy and sell enough homes, especially in the same area, to develop a relationship with a specific title agent.

Unless you have a title agent you have used in the past and feel comfortable with, it's okay to let the realtor pick the agent. As I mentioned earlier, it's about relationships and communication. If your realtor has a relationship with an agent he or she can trust, go with it. I do suggest you meet the agent so that you can feel comfortable with him or her. I've had some bad experiences with title agents my realtor has picked; however, realtors almost always make the right choice.

Realtors are anxious to pick your title company because they get kickbacks. Not kickbacks in the traditional definition of the word,

caution Many production homebuilders have their own title companies and strongly insist that you use them. If not using your own agent presents a problem for you, you need to have that conversation with the production homebuilder's sales agent up front. He or she will make an exception. If you don't have a strong preference, use the homebuilder's title company. All title companies provide protection and will manage your funds properly.

but they do get many perks—anything from free business cards and letterhead, free postage on mailers, and free pizza parties to trips to Las Vegas. To be fair, it's more of a finder's fee. Does this affect you? Yes! Usually, you get better service and pricing from a title company that has a relationship with a seasoned realtor. It's all legal and works out to your benefit.

If you don't have a personal relationship with a title agent, it's okay to go with a recommendation from your realtor, especially because feeling comfortable with the title agent is important. Don't forget that even if your realtor does pick the title company and agent, that agent still works for you. You're paying the agent, so he or she should keep your best interests in mind at all times.

Also, don't forget to ask your realtor to negotiate the title company's prices. You don't have to pay the full amount on all the title company's fees. Many of these fees are fixed, but many are not. Remember: You can negotiate almost any expense involved in buying or building your new home. From the contractor's costs and house appraisal to title fees and realtor commissions, *negotiate*.

NEGOTIATE EVERYTHING

I can't emphasize the necessity of negotiation enough. It's the only way you'll always get the best price. While preparing for this chapter, I wanted to see just how far I could take this negotiating thing. I went to Sears and tried to negotiate on a washer and dryer. Sears, a retail store. After only a few minutes, I negotiated $100 off the retail price of those two appliances. That savings was certainly worth 15 minutes of speaking with the sales rep. You don't have to pay retail just because it's marked that way.

What Does a Title Company Do for You?

A title company works for you and is paid by you. The purpose of a title company is to be sure that your property is free of any hidden problems—that is, clear of debt, liens, encumbrances, encroachments, adverse possession, eminent domain, easements, and so forth. Title companies are there to protect you and your investment. They make sure your neighbor's garage isn't built on your property, ensure that a previous owner didn't lose the property in a poker game or to the IRS, and warn you about easements or other factors that can affect your property's value or resale. They issue you a *title policy*, which is an actual insurance policy.

ADVERSE POSSESSION

I'm sure you're wondering how a neighbor could build his garage on your property. It actually happened on the first home I bought. The owner of the house I was buying built his garage 2 feet away from his property line. When the neighbor decided to build his garage adjacent to the owner's, the owner suggested he add it onto his garage and use his exterior wall as a common wall. This meant the new garage was built two feet over the neighbor's property line to connect with the owner's existing garage. That was fine in 1935 when the garages were built. Today, that's called an encroachment and requires a notarized addendum to your deed of trust recognizing it. In the example of the neighbor's garage, if that encroachment hadn't been recognized legally, the owner's property under the neighbor's garage and the entire length of the neighbor's driveway would have become his property. The neighbor then owns that land forever. This is called *adverse possession*.

In adverse possession, traditional common law provides a method for someone to obtain title (ownership) to land simply through use. The common-law rules for adverse possession have been recognized under both federal and state statutes. A typical statute allows a person to get title to land from the actual owner simply by using the land out in the open for all to see. Another common example is your neighbor building a fence on your land with the intention of taking the property, and you knew about it but did nothing. If this continued for a period of time set by state law, your neighbor might be able to claim this property as his or her own. The theory is that by not disputing your neighbor's use of your property through a lawsuit, you, the actual owner, have abandoned your rights to the property.

I mention easements because of my experience with them. An *easement* is a strip of land going through your property that allows someone else access to your property to service or install a utility. Usually an easement is straightforward and gives, for example, the water company access to a water main that runs in front of your house under your property. You own the land, but the water company has the right to run a bulldozer across that strip to dig it up if need be—with or without your permission.

I purchased a home in California a few years ago, and when I read the title report, I discovered 21 separate easements on my property. The title company included a map outlining each one. Twenty-one easements was bad enough, but all the easements ran down the center of my property, through my living room, and out my dining room. It seemed that 20 or so years earlier, the city decided that when it ran utilities into that area, it would use the ridge line of the mountain to do it. Over the years, the city eventually built a major road in the valley and ran all the utilities along that road. No one ever went back to do the work to remove the old easements.

When I saw the potential for water lines, cable TV, gas, storm water, electric, sewer, telephone, fiber-optics, and who knows what else, I was shocked. Unfortunately, the title company I chose was not looking out for me. When I called a company representative, he told me not to worry; the city would never use the easements. I explained that as long as they were part of my deed and title, the city could.

It took more than two months of arguing with the title company to fight with the city engineers while I was in a different state to get the city to remove the easements. I'm sure the easements would never have been a problem, but if they had, the title company would have had to pay for any damages incurred. I just felt a lot better forcing the title company to give me a "clean" title, free of any encumbrances.

The title company is also responsible for escrow (or holding back your money) to pay the seller, property taxes, first month's mortgage payment, HOA fees, and the entire funds of the transaction until it's complete. The fee the company charges you (which is negotiable) is for this research and money handling.

> **tip** Easements are as important with new homes and undeveloped property as they are with an existing home on a developed piece of land. Undeveloped property often has easements and right-of-ways already on it because no structures are in the way. Also, many recently subdivided pieces of land need easements to get utilities to the new homes. So read your title report and be sure your property is free and clear.

WHAT IS ESCROW?

Escrow is depositing money or documents from a real estate transaction with an impartial third party (escrow agent) that are to be disbursed to the rightful parties when all conditions of the transaction have been met. That means the title company acts as a liaison between the buyer and the seller to hold all monies throughout the transaction; pay any fees, costs, and taxes; and be sure of the proper and legal final disbursements of all funds.

What's the Relationship Between Your Realtor and Your Title Agent?

The relationship between your realtor and title agent is one of sales—not so much the sale of your home, but the realtor generating business for the title company. Realtors are on the front line of sales, and the title company relies on realtors to bring them business. Often, title companies offer sales and business support to realtors in the form of business cards, letterhead, mailing lists, websites, limos for open houses, and other marketing tools. This support is in exchange for realtors sending them business. Is this arrangement legal? Yes, as long as no cash has been exchanged.

Many states have laws that prohibit realtors from accepting cash from title companies; however, marketing support is perfectly legal and ethical. Personally, I like when a realtor has a relationship with a title company as long as the realtor remembers to look out for me. I am the client. I'm paying the realtor, not the title company. As long as he protects me with the lowest title fees, I'm okay with them having a business relationship. Many times I relied on my realtor to work out a problem with my escrow or another part of the transaction with the title company. Because of their relationship, the problem was handled quickly and efficiently. The title agent wants to maintain a trusted, profitable relationship with a realtor that took time and money to develop.

If you transact many real estate deals per year and have built a relationship with a title agent you feel comfortable with, by all means use that agent. Just tell your realtor up front that you would like to use your own title agent.

Code of Ethics and Conduct

If you're curious about whether realtors have a code of ethics and standards of practice, you can find it at http://www.realtor.org/mempolweb.nsf/pages/printable2005Code.

At the time of publishing, I could not find a code of ethics for the banking industry. It seems that every individual bank has its own or none at all. The same is true for title companies.

Here's a typical code of conduct that CitiBank uses:

http://www.citigroup.com/citigroup/corporategovernance/data/codeconduct_en.pdf

The American Banking Association has the following information and link:

"In the aftermath of Enron and a flood of similar corporate misdeeds, the ethical conduct of public companies and their executives has become the subject of intense scrutiny and far-reaching legislation.

The Sarbanes Oxley Act of 2002 mandated the adoption of codes of ethics at publicly traded companies. Recently revised listing standards of the stock exchanges have expanded greatly and so has the required actions a company must now take. The banking industry has long been the object of business relationships built on high ethical practices. The recent focus on corporate ethical behavior compels a fresh look at your organization's policies, procedures, and practices" (http://www.sarbanes-oxley.com/).

Of the three professional organizations mentioned previously—lenders, title companies, and realtors—real estate is the only industry that requires state certification, license, and continuing education in all 50 states. Even to maintain a license, realtors must complete 24 hours of state-certified continuing education units (CEUs) every 24 months.

Currently, title agents and lenders in many states have no requirements or regulation whatsoever, but there's a move afoot to require licensing for both professions. Residential mortgage brokers are most likely going to be the first required by each state to be educated, licensed, and bonded. This move is being driven by the real estate industry as a whole. Realtors, contractors, courts, homebuyers, homesellers, and state regulatory agencies are all asking for legislature protecting the consumer through licensing.

note States now require their realtors to have been trained by a state-certified school and certified instructors in certified classes. These classes include three hours of contract law, three hours of agency law, three hours of commissioner's standards, three hours of legal issues, three hours of fair housing practices, three hours of disclosure rules, and six hours of miscellaneous or general credit. These requirements can vary from state to state.

At the publication of this book, the following are the number of states requiring residential mortgage brokers to be educated and licensed[1]:

- *Registration and/or licensing and education required*   19 states
- *Registration and/or licensing, but no education required at this time*   11 states
- *Course approval in process*   8 states
- *Does not regulate mortgage lenders*   12 states

Licensing for title agents is running a close second to residential mortgage broker licensing, with a little less than half the United States requiring licensing and education. The trend strongly suggests that in a few years, both professions will be regulated.

[1]Information provided by http://www.schoolofmortgagelending.com.

Summary

This chapter has explained how to identify and choose good realtors, discover what their hot buttons are, find out how they think, and see how they can help you find your property and maybe even your builder. You learned how to choose a good lender and how to work with him or her to maximize your loan amount while minimizing your interest rate.

You also discovered what a title company does for you; learned to understand the relationship between you, your realtor, and the title agent; and looked at the industry code of ethics and conduct for your professionals.

Besides your builder, your realtor, lender, and title agent are the ones who will make your project a success. They can help you find land and money, and make sure it's all done correctly and safely so that you can enjoy your new home for as long as you keep it.

Doing Your "Home" Work on Your Homebuilder

6

You need to do your "home" work on your homebuilder. He's the one who's responsible for the entire construction of your new home and helps you coordinate everything about your new home. Your relationship with him is the most important one you'll have throughout the construction process. You need to interview, thoroughly qualify, and feel comfortable with the homebuilder you choose because you'll be spending a lot of time with him over the next nine months to a year.

I know, you've heard that a "good homebuilder" is an oxymoron. That's not the case. Most every licensed, insured homebuilder or general contractor is a good one. Otherwise, they couldn't stay in business long enough to pass the contractor's license qualifications, earn enough money to pay for their insurances, and feed their families. Unfortunately, the only homebuilders you ever hear about are the bad ones. Bad homebuilders have a tendency to weed themselves out quickly. Don't forget: Even the good ones make mistakes and have problems beyond their control. It's how they solve those problems that keep them in business. Nearly all of a homebuilder's business comes from referrals.

In this chapter:

* Learn how to find a homebuilder in your geographic area
* Put your building candidates to the test with professional trade and licensing agencies
* Check up on your potential homebuilder by speaking with previous clients
* Speak with your homebuilder's subcontractors to see whether they are financially stable

To do list

- ☐ Ask everyone you know if he or she can recommend a good homebuilder.
- ☐ Speak with realtors who sell in the area where you plan to build.
- ☐ Speak with homebuilders who are building new homes in the area where you plan to build.
- ☐ Meet with them in their own environment.
- ☐ Bring your accordion file.
- ☐ Check business licensing and trade associations.
- ☐ Check with your homebuilder's previous clients, *not* clients on his referral list.
- ☐ Speak with a few of the homebuilder's subcontractors.
- ☐ Go with your intuition. If you have a good feeling about a homebuilder and no one you've talked to has any concerns about him, he's probably the right person to build your home.

The Process of Finding a Good Homebuilder

Finding a good homebuilder is as easy as finding a good dentist or a good doctor, if not easier. If you're thinking that finding a good dentist or doctor isn't that easy, don't worry. You definitely need to do a little research and some legwork to talk to a few people, but this effort pays big dividends when you find the best homebuilder for your needs. This chapter takes you step by step through the process of finding a good builder.

First, you learn how to look for a homebuilder in your area, near where you want to build your new home, and then you see how to find out if he's the right homebuilder for you.

How to Locate a Homebuilder Near Your Location

The first step in the process, of course, is to find a few homebuilders to interview. You can look in the yellow pages or on the Internet, but this information doesn't tell you whether a homebuilder builds in the location where you want your new home. It also doesn't tell you

caution In Chapter 5, "Building Your Team of Professionals," you learned that some homebuilders won't work with realtors or pay only a flat $500 commission. This might affect your realtor's performance or could add a commission expense to your new home. Be aware of this issue when conversing with your potential homebuilder and realtor.

whether he's a good homebuilder and whether past clients would recommend him.

To begin the process, start by asking everyone you know whether he or she can recommend a good homebuilder or knows of anyone who might. Tell them you're planning to build or buy a new home and see who has suggestions for you. Get their recommendations. Ask your friends, neighbors, co-workers, people at your church or associations, and others who have built their own custom homes. Talk with realtors, contact your local contracting school, and drive around. Driving around is the same way you're going to find your "dirt" (building location). You learn more about locating a homebuilder by finding the land in Chapter 7, "How to Select Property Properly."

> **note** Most local builder's associations have computerized databases listing builder members by areas and price ranges. A simple phone call to the association can provide an instant list of homebuilder information. Additionally, although hiring a builder who's a member of the local builder's association doesn't ensure that the builder is a good one, it's a strong indication that the builder supports the construction industry on a professional level, is involved with the best in the industry, and has a plethora of avenues and resources to solve problems.

HOW LONG DOES IT TAKE TO BUILD A HOUSE?

The process of building a custom home can be completed in about nine months on average. A good homebuilder can build a custom home in six months if everything goes exactly right, but nine months is more likely. Many factors determine how quickly or slowly your home can be built. Nearly all these factors are out of your homebuilder's control. The causes for delays can include the following:

- *Weather, such as rain, snow, and frost*   Even if the weather looks great and the sun is shining, the ground might still be frozen or too wet to pour your concrete (flatwork). Often homeowners get upset when they don't see any activity on a bright sunny day.

- *Material deliveries, such as custom-order tile, or custom-made materials, such as kitchen cabinets*   Custom materials are often back-ordered, which can delay part of the building process and consequently affect other tasks. Tile is a good example. Many high-end marble floor and wall tiles come from Italy and Indonesia. If the U.S. distributor is out of stock of the tile you chose, your project could be delayed.

   Cabinetry is a good example of custom-made items causing delays. Most kitchen cabinets are made for your specific home. They can't be started until the drywall is finished and can take between 6 and 12 weeks to complete. If kitchen cabinets aren't installed on time, countertops can't be measured and custom made. If countertops aren't installed, the kitchen sink can't be installed, and on it goes.

- *Subdivision approval, such as roads, utilities, and right-of-ways* These administrative factors are also out of your homebuilder's control. For a single home, subdivision approval usually isn't an issue, but in a neighborhood with two or more homes being built, the city, town, or county needs to inspect to make sure the infrastructure is complete. The infrastructure includes utilities (water, telephone, sewer, and cable TV), storm water drainage, green areas and parks, traffic control (lights) and street-lights, water meters, and road design. All these elements need to be up to code. If not, the governing municipality won't approve subdividing and building on the land, even though the builder is allowed to begin construction.

- *Scheduling of subcontractors* Everyone is familiar with waiting for a plumber or electrician who doesn't show up. The same thing happens on a new home construction project, only on a larger scale. The homebuilder is responsible for making sure all the many subcontractors not only show up, but also show up at the exact time they're needed. If a plumber shows up before the countertops are installed, the homebuilder has to reschedule the plumber, which can be difficult because often the plumber is already scheduled to work on another job. This means the entire job could wait until the plumber can reschedule the work. Also, many subcontractors won't work on the home if other subs are there because they think they'll get in each other's way. In this situation, often they just leave the job site, which is why under some circumstances, it could take more than a year to complete your new home.

Does Your Homebuilder Pass the Test?

After you have selected a few homebuilders, schedule a time for interviewing them. Set up the interviews in their offices or their homes to get a good idea of how organized they are. Also, they will be most comfortable in their

tip Ask the homebuilder to *please not answer the phone while you're there.* If you don't, every 10 minutes, you'll be interrupted with a 10-minute call.

own environment. They'll speak more easily and have access to more samples and ideas than if they meet you in a restaurant or at your home.

In Chapter 9, "Know What's Included in the Base Price," I describe the value of creating an accordion file with all your design ideas, photographs, and brochures. Bring that accordion file with your floor plan ideas so that you can communicate your basic ideas to him. This way, the homebuilder can speak specifically to the design elements you're looking for, such as stone exteriors, fireplaces, architectural bump-outs around doors and windows, cobblestone driveways, or whatever. You can listen to his interpretations of your ideas to see how well you communicate with each other. This process should give you a good idea of how you well you'll be able to communicate over the next nine months to a year.

Check Business Licensing and Trade Associations

One way you can check up on your potential homebuilder is by contacting government agencies that license builders and their businesses. You can start by contacting your local Better Business Bureau (BBB).

However, the BBB might not provide the amount of information you need to decide on your potential homebuilder. The BBB has information on your homebuilder only if he's a member of the local BBB or someone in that town filed a complaint against him. Most metropolitan areas have several individual BBBs, some as many as 35. Your area might have fewer than that; nonetheless, checking with all individual BBBs can take a lot of time and effort. Most homebuilders favor a particular area but will build anywhere within a 50-mile radius of their office. You would have to identify every BBB, get the phone numbers, and call each one. You might want to start with the town or city where the homebuilder does most of his building and work outward in concentric circles, checking a half dozen or so BBBs.

The best way to be sure your potential homebuilder is licensed, in good standing, and free of professional claims against him is to check with your state's Registrar of Contractors (ROC) or Contractors State License Board. Every state has one. California's website is http://www.cslb.ca.gov/, Arizona's is http://www.rc.state.az.us, Nevada's is http://www.nscb.state.nv.us, and Illinois's is http://www.dpr.state.il.us/licenselookup/default.asp, for example. To find your state requirements and websites, go to http://www.contractors-license.org. It's a good starting point for this information.

As the public information officer for the Port of San Diego and the San Diego International Airport, I often started press conferences with the statement "We're the government. We're here to help you!" This opening always lightened the mood. Also, when I teach this subject in real estate school, I mention what Will Rogers said: "Be thankful we're not getting all the government we're paying for."

In the case of your state's contractor-licensing departments, all that government *is* good for you, the homebuyer. Did you know that in Arizona, a contractor must be bonded and insured and pass trade and business-management tests before becoming a licensed contractor? And that a state-issued license is required for any jobs that total or exceed $750, including labor and materials? And that a homeowner can receive up to $30,000 to finish or repair faulty workmanship caused by a contractor or subcontractor?

Here's an example of how Arizona's Registrar of Contractors works to protect homeowners in that state. The following table lists some statistics from Arizona's ROC for 2004.

Arizona Registrar of Contractors Statistics for 2004

Revoked licenses	1,006
Suspended licenses	417
Inspections to resolve complaints	728
Payouts to homeowners	$4,800,000
Average payout	$9,591
New contractor applications processed per year	7,200
Contractor renewals per year	18,000
Managed contractor's licenses	50,700
Unlicensed contractor arrest warrants	1,000
Filed criminal cases	575
Complaint investigations	2,906
Current staff	138

Source: *The Arizona Republic*, October 31, 2004

How about that!

Check with Your Homebuilder's Previous Clients

If you ask your homebuilder for a list of previous clients, he'll supply it happily. Keep in mind, however, that this list is a lot like personal references given to potential employers—most people don't include the name and phone number of the jerk who fired them when they told him off. The same is true for a homebuilder. The names on his list include only past clients he can trust to give good recommendations. You should still speak with them, however, and ask them the following questions:

- Did they have many problems during the course of construction? What kind of problems?

- How well did the homebuilder fix any problems? Did he fix them quickly? Who paid for the repairs?

- Were you satisfied with the homebuilder's overall quality of work?

- Did your home come in under, on, or over budget?

- Was the homebuilder receptive to your changes during the course of construction (change orders)?

note Everybody has problems while building a new home. It's a complicated task. Just because a client had problems during the construction of his or her home doesn't necessarily mean the builder involved is a bad one. It's how a homebuilder responds to and fixes problems that is important. Remember: It's the homebuilder's responsibility to fix all problems before you accept your new home.

- Did the builder communicate with you during the course of construction? Did he explain the process and answer your questions to your satisfaction? Did he ensure that his subcontractors were responsive to your requests, if applicable?
- How well did the homebuilder respond to warranty issues?

The answers to these questions should generate conversations that give you insight on how that homebuilder works and handles adversity. After a few of these conversations, you'll get a good idea of the type of problems that came up and how they were handled. No homebuilder gets a perfect recommendation, even from his best customers.

Before you leave, ask the homeowners on the reference list if they know of other homes in their area your potential homebuilder has built. Look around the neighborhood for other homes similar in architectural design and floor plan. Knock on those doors and talk with those homeowners, too. Most likely your homebuilder has built those homes. Often a homebuilder builds an entire street of homes, but he might not have included names of all those homeowners on his reference list. Find out why.

When you do talk with other homeowners who weren't included on the homebuilder's reference list, take what they say with a grain of salt. The reason they weren't on the reference list might not be a problem that was the homebuilder's fault, or the reason could have been an issue that couldn't be resolved to everyone's satisfaction. It might be the cause of the homebuilder, the homeowner, or just circumstances. In the building industry, as with any sales-related industry, you learn quickly that you just can't please everyone all the time, no matter what you do. Keep this in mind when checking on your homebuilder's references.

Listen to What Your Homebuilder's Subs Can Tell You

When my clients or students ask me for a litmus test of a homebuilder's financial stability, I tell them about a trick that most homebuilders hate. If you want to know how secure your future is with your potential homebuilder, ask him for the contact information of one or two of his subcontractors, such as his electrician, plumber, or framer. The homebuilder might be apprehensive about giving you this information because generally he doesn't want homeowners communicating with his subcontractors. It's not because he has anything to hide. It's because he doesn't want homeowners giving the subs direction, asking for anything that might be contrary to his arrangements with his subs, or adding items to the construction without them being added to the specs and eventually the final bill.

After you have assured your potential homebuilder that you won't let that happen, he'll part with a few numbers. Now here it comes—the information most homebuilders don't want you to know: To find out whether your potential homebuilder has the financial security and the integrity you're looking for, ask each sub, "Does the homebuilder pay you on time?"

Subs might seem confused by this question, but in most cases they'll answer it. Usually they say that the homebuilder is a little late in his payments but good about paying them after a while—sometimes 60 days after the project or after a few faxes or phone calls but no later than that. The other typical answer is that it's always months before the homebuilder pays them, and even then, often payments aren't for the full amount contracted but are only partial payments. Subs continue to work for homebuilders who pay late or partially only because they're afraid that if they don't, they'll never hear from them again.

Most homebuilders pay late, but this is okay as long as they aren't often extremely late (usually by more than a couple months) or renege on paying their subs at all. Holding their money to make the maximum interest until the last moment is one thing, but sometimes they're borrowing from Peter to pay Paul, which is an indication that they could be in financial trouble. You don't want to contract with a homebuilder facing serious financial woes. If the story you get from a homebuilder's subs appears to point that way, you should take a pass on that homebuilder and keep looking.

Look at it this way: Most homebuilders become homebuilders because they like to, well, build, not because they are necessarily good business managers or accountants. If they were good at accounting, they would have become accountants! Many small-scale homebuilders usually don't know what it costs them to build a house until after they turn over the keys to a homeowner. Generally, they aren't good at keeping track of their costs. This won't affect you because as the homeowner, you have a agreed-on contractual sales price. It does affect a homebuilder's profit margins, however.

The homebuilders you hear about disappearing or going out of business get too far behind financially and get into trouble by doing things such as taking the deposit for their next home to pay the electrician on the home they built four months ago. If they've overextended themselves on the past two or three homes they've built and dug themselves in too deeply, they could go under while building your home. You have probably heard horror stories about homebuilders stealing their customers' money and running off in the middle of the job and the night, but this is actually quite rare. Speaking with a few subs goes a long way toward ensuring that you don't end up with one of those homebuilders.

Don't Panic: Interviewing Is Much Easier Than It Sounds

All this interviewing probably sounds like a lot of work, but it's only a few phone calls and an evening or two visiting your homebuilder's referrals and talking to a few of his subs. I can promise you that spending a few hours checking up on potential homebuilders is a lot easier than running into problems during the course of construction. Evaluate your conversations and go with your instincts. This process also gives you a much higher level of confidence when working with your homebuilder. Don't forget: This is the man who will be spending a quarter of a million or more of your dollars over the next year. Be sure he's someone you can trust to do that and someone you can communicate with easily.

Don't be afraid to knock on doors. If you're shy, you might not like the idea of approaching a homebuilder's clients out of the blue to ask them questions, but the effort is worth it. Start with only one door. Most people you meet will love to talk with you. When was the last time you mentioned how pretty someone's new baby is or asked about someone's new car or job? People are always glad when someone is genuinely interested in a topic that's important to them. The same is true when asking people about their homes. Show a genuine interest in their homes, and they'll love to talk with you about them.

Try it just one time to see how much fun it can be and how much you'll learn about the homebuilder and the building process. You'll hear first-hand about what homeowners liked and what they didn't. You'll hear all about the dos and don'ts. Remember that you and the homeowners you talk to already have a lot in common: a new dream home. It can be exciting to speak with someone about the biggest project going on in both your lives, and I'll bet you make a few friends in the process.

Summary

This chapter has explained how to find a homebuilder in your geographic area and who to speak with to get references. You learned how to put your building candidates to the test with professional trade and licensing agencies to help ensure that you work with a homebuilder you can trust.

You also learned how to check up on potential homebuilders by interviewing previous clients about their experiences. In addition, speaking with your homebuilder's subcontractors can tell you a lot about your potential homebuilder's professional ethics, communication skills, and financial stability.

Part II

Getting Started

How to Select Property Properly

7

This chapter discusses how to find your dirt. In the United States today, finding land you want to build on is becoming more difficult. Don't get me wrong: There's still plenty of land, but it's in the badlands of Wyoming or the swamps of Louisiana. Alaska has a lot of land for reasonable prices, too. Finding a good, inexpensive piece of property in an area with good school districts and an easy commute to work is getting nearly impossible, however. In the desirable parts of the country, suburbs are becoming less accessible and are moving farther out. Subdivisions and shopping centers are being built in areas that only the most daring farmers were willing to go to just a few years ago.

I did, however, say "nearly impossible." There are still parcels of land hidden between occupied homes in neighborhoods 10 to 20 years old. You can still find what's called *horse property* sitting on one to five acres that are in the process of being subdivided into half-acre or one-acre lots to be built on. Even larger tracts of land, such as farms, dairies, flower fields, hay and vegetable fields, and vineyards, are slowly being sold off in small pieces or in their entirety. Be creative with how and where you look for your next piece of land.

In this chapter:

* Learn that the property doesn't always come with the house
* Understand the many questions you must ask before buying a piece of land
* Explore how to find a piece of property because the dirt won't come to you
* Find out how to use realtors, friends, colleagues, and family to find your property
* To find out how to download a list of interview questions, see page 4

Who Supplies the Land and Who Doesn't

Whether you buy the dirt separately is a function of what type of home you're going to buy or build. Many people who are building a custom home start with the land and build up from there. They buy the land because of the price, its location, and often its view. If you already own the land, a custom/semi-custom homebuilder comes in and builds without a second thought. The homebuilder's focus is on the house itself. It doesn't matter to him who owns the land. So whether you already own the land or want to go out and buy the land yourself doesn't affect your ability to have a custom or semi-custom home built on it.

If you're buying a previously owned or production home, of course, the land is included in the home's price. If you're planning to build a custom or semi-custom home, you can own the land before you select your homebuilder, the land can be included with your new home by the homebuilder, or the land can be included by your homebuilder or his realtor as a separate transaction. You need to discuss this issue with your homebuilder when you interview him. Whether you're buying the land yourself or from the homebuilder, you need to do some "home" work on the land.

The following section offers a helpful list of questions you need to ask before buying your new land to protect your investment and maintain your expected quality of life.

Asking All the Right Questions Helps You Buy Better Property

You need to ask all the following questions when you're buying land:

- How much does the land cost? Is it a good value for its size, type, and location? What are the land's comps?

- What's the size of the parcel? Is it big enough to build the home you want and still have room for the pool, out-buildings, rodeo corral, whatever?

- Are there buildings, wells, barns, other structure, or debris that need to be demolished, filled in, dug up, or hauled off? If so, at whose expense?

- Where is the land located? Do you need to pack a cooler of food, water, and a sleeping bag to go see it? Is it a reasonable distance from, well, anything?

> **tip**
> Remember comps from Chapter 5, "Building Your Team of Professionals"? The property's comps (comparable values) is only a starting point, or asking price. Remember to do some "home" work and know the per acre, per half acre, or per square foot value of a parcel of land and negotiate.

- How close is the land to the freeway or a major road? Will it take you 2 hours to commute to work? And will the traffic noise keep you awake at night if the land is *too* close to a major road?

- How close is the land to necessary services, such as an airport, food shopping, gas stations, auto repair, and drugstores? Being far away from these services can be a huge inconvenience when you need a quart of milk, the tank of gas you forgot the night before, or a midnight prescription when your child is sick. And where is the closest hospital, just in case?

- What municipality is the land in (incorporated township or unincorporated county)? Towns and cities have different building codes and vary widely in taxes and services provided.

- What are the school and municipal taxes in that area? A county is usually much less expensive than towns and cities, but offers fewer services, such as nearby schools, and might have one sheriff with 400 square miles to patrol instead of four police offers covering one town, for example.

- What type of soil do you have: clay, sand, rock? A septic system might cost two to three times as much in clay soil because of poor drainage, and rock could add $10,000 to $100,000 to the construction cost if blasting is necessary to get your house in.

- Is the land flat, sloping, or mountain-goat terrain? This factor significantly affects the construction cost and design of your new home.

- Speaking of mountain goats, are there protected species on the land, such as frogs, newts, owls, or even particular trees and other flora? Does the property have coyotes? I lived in two areas of the country where coyotes ate all my household pets!

tip Check on snow removal, trash pickup, fire services, emergency medical, school bus stops, and streetlights, too. An unincorporated area most likely won't have streetlights. No streetlights can make sleeping easier, but they do provide a measure of safety and security.

caution Don't try to build a one-story California ranch house on a property that slopes 50 feet from front to back. Even a raised ranch on a flat piece of land with a daylight basement (partially aboveground) can be a problem. On land with large grade changes or slopes, building certain architectural styles can be difficult or impossible. The most commonly built home, the California ranch, is designed as a one-story home and needs to be on a flat piece of property. Even a raised ranch or split-level ranch doesn't allow enough change in elevation (side view) of the house design to compensate for the change in the land's elevation. If the property does have large grade changes, you have to consider another architectural style for your new home. If changing the architectural style isn't an option, you need to specify that to your realtor when selecting property.

- Does the land have water (both drinking water brought to the property and problem drainage water that you want to get away from the property)? Both types of water can represent a huge expense. Do you have to bring town or county water lines onto your property? If so, how far and what will it cost? Do you have to drill a deep well? If so, how deep and how much will it cost? What's the depth of the water table during all four seasons and during drought conditions? What is the quality of the water?

> **note** I lived in a beautiful neighborhood in Washington State on community well water. After I bought, I found out that I couldn't sell my house because the well water contained low concentrations of nitrates caused by all the years of agricultural fertilizers used in that area. This is a big problem in northern California, too. If you're curious how I solved that one, email me from my website at http://www.LonSafko.com.

- Is the land in a floodplain? Does the property flood? Will your new home flood? How well does it drain? Is a stream going through the land? Can I divert it? Will the Federal Wetlands Act allow me to move it? If your property has any state- or federal-sanctioned wetlands, you can't add any runoff or disturb any land within 150 feet of their edges.

- Is there a city sewer or will I require a septic system at the property? Clay soil can double or triple the size of your septic system and leach fields.

- Is there cable television, or will I need a satellite dish? This factor affects cost and inconvenience to you.

- Can I get cell phone service in that area? In a blackout during a storm, cell phones might be the only phones working, as most home phones now are wireless with a base station that goes dead when the electricity is lost.

> **tip** Get at least one non-wireless phone that plugs directly into the wall in case of a power outage. These phones work on between 42.5 to 56.5 volts direct current provided by large batteries at the phone company and still work if the electricity goes out, unless they require electricity for their base.

- Is there electricity, natural gas, telephone, and cable already on the property, or will you have to pay to get it there? In rural areas, some property could be 1,000 feet or more from the street where the closest utilities are. Utility poles and transformers are expensive and need to be considered.

- Are there any easements, right-of-ways, eminent domain, encroachments, or adverse possessions? For a reminder on these factors, refer to Chapter 5, "Building Your Team of Professionals."

- Is any future construction planned, such as freeways, commercial warehouses, drug rehabilitation hospitals, or prisons? Not that I'm against any of them, but they do affect your resale value and ability to sell.

- Is the land in a historic area? This can severely limit what you can build and dramatically increase the cost of building to historic compliance.

- Are there any existing structures? Are there any structures you can use, or do they have to be demolished and removed?

- What is the zoning, not only for your property, but also the surrounding property?

- What are the zoning requirements? Most zoning requirements allow your neighbor's home to be built 10 feet away from your property line. Some codes restrict you from building a two-story home so that you don't block your neighbor's view.

- What's the neighborhood like? What kinds of houses are there? Will yours fit in? What if you're surrounded on three sides by dairies? How will that geodesic dome house next to your property affect your resale value?

- What's the closest commercial property, and what kind of business is on it? Look at this question from the perspective of noise, traffic, and air, ground water, and light pollution.

- Ask to see the title report, the perk test for the septic system (see Chapter 20, "What You Need to Know About Your New Septic System"), the soil or hydrologic report for the well, and a zoning map. When I purchase a new home, I go to the town, ask these questions, and even visit and walk around the school my daughter will attend so that I can meet the principal.

note You don't want any surprises, such as the one I had when I purchased my home in California. Shortly thereafter, the town approved two half-million-square-feet warehouse distribution centers adjacent to my neighborhood. My neighbors and I had been told a state-managed wildlife preserve was in that area. After construction began, the peaceful serenity of chirping birds was replaced by the chirping of backup alarms on semi-tractor trailers at the loading docks all day.

tip Yes, light pollution. If the building, such as a shopping center or warehouse, has parking lot lights or security lighting, be sure your potential bedroom windows are shielded from them. Make sure security lighting is on a motion sensor so that it comes on only when needed and doesn't burn all night.

- Does or will the property have a homeowner's association (HOA)? What are its restrictions? Most HOAs restrict the colors you can use, dictate the square footage of grass lawn, specify the number and size of trees in your yard, and even decide whether you can put a flag out.

- What are the CC&Rs? CC&Rs are the covenants, conditions, and restrictions filed along with your deed of trust that specify how you use you property. As with an HOA, CC&Rs specify what colors you can paint your house, whether you can have TV antennas and clotheslines, whether you can plant winter grass, whether you can have boats or cars in storage and own motor homes, and so on. CC&Rs can be 20 to 40 pages of restrictions. If they exist, you better read them before you buy. They are legal and binding.

ALWAYS ASK WHETHER NATURAL DISASTERS ARE COMMON

When inspecting a potential property purchase, you should ask about all forms of natural disasters you need to consider. When I lived in California near a wildlife preserve, I needed to worry about wildfires. (Remember the Scripps Ranch fire a few years ago, when more than 300 homes were destroyed or damaged by wildfire?) I also worried about landslides and mudslides and losing my backyard during heavy rains. And if that wasn't enough, I worried constantly about earthquakes. My dad and sister who live in Ft. Myers and my son in Tampa, Florida: Hurricanes, anyone? My brother in Denver: How about a few blizzards and a dozen tornados each year? My daughter in San Diego on the Del Mar coast: Can anyone spell *tsunami*? These concerns shouldn't be a source of constant worry, but you do need to play "what if" and take them into consideration. The brushfire issue caught me by surprise when my homeowner's insurance company canceled my policy when it discovered my property backed up to a canyon. The new insurance company charged me a premium to insure that house.

Finding the Best Piece of Land for You

Time to get back to finding the dirt. The best way to find both a piece of land and a good builder is to drive around the area you want to live in. You've done the research on or are familiar with approximately where you want to live. Take a methodical approach to driving around the area. First, put together a property search kit that consists of these items:

- A road map of the area that you can draw on
- A highlighter
- A cell phone
- A pad of paper and pen
- A full tank of gas
- Plenty of coffee (I'm sure I'm not the only one who needs this)

Now head out, and make a fun day of it. Take yourself out to lunch for a much-needed break.

Start in any area on the map and drive up one street and down the other. Here's what you are looking for: a house that's under construction or recently completed or a vacant piece of land. With your property search kit at hand, you have a complete mobile office. When you see a "For Sale" sign, a "Custom Homes By" sign, or realtor's sign, make a call to the homebuilder or realtor listed on the sign. On a weekend or holiday, you usually get the homebuilder's answering machine at his office. The weekend is catch-up time for homebuilders, so leave a message. They'll call you back the next business day. With realtors, you might get their cell phones or pagers and be able to speak with them immediately. If you get their voicemail, they usually call you back within 15 minutes.

Ask some preliminary questions about the property. Start with the price. The answer to this question either prompts the next question or concludes your conversation. When you speak with the homebuilder, ask for addresses of other homes in the area he has built so that you can drive by those homes to see whether you like his work. If you do, call him back and schedule a time to meet with him. Don't set the meeting between 6 a.m. and 4 p.m., however. Schedule time with him in the evening or on the weekend when he can focus on you and your needs, not the constant ring of his cell phone.

Scour the area. If you see a vacant piece of land with no sign, stop your car, talk to the neighbors, get the scoop on the land, and get the owner's information. You'd be surprised how much you can find out from the neighbors, and you'll get to meet your new neighbors if you decide to build there, which can be a good thing or a warning.

Also, write down the address and a description, and draw a circle around the property on your map. When you get home, do a little Internet research. You might be surprised at what you find.

GRAPHIC INFORMATION SYSTEM

Most counties now have a *graphic information system* (*GIS*). If you search the Internet for your county's tax assessor's office, you might find its system. If you do, you can type in an address or see a map of your county. When you click on the area you're interested in, the map zooms in on the property. When you select that parcel, the information box fills up with everything you ever wanted to know about the property: the name and address of who owns it, the current taxes, the meets and bounds (the surveyor's description using bearings and distances to describe that property exactly), square footage or acres, and even neighbors' information. In most cases, there's even a link that takes you to the recorded deed of trust, which tells you how much the owner paid for the land and when it was purchased.

Here's the link for Maricopa County, Arizona: http://www.maricopa.gov/Assessor/GIS/map.html. Take a look, play around and have some fun, and then go find the website for your county!

Realtors Can Help You Find Your Land

Speak with realtors to help you find your land. Remember, when you're buying a new home or property, you don't have to stick with one realtor. You don't have to sign a buying contract, only a selling contract. You can work with a dozen different realtors at once. Get the word out. Have five or six different realtors emailing you about all the possibilities. It's like having your own sales force working for you.

Email is a great way to work with realtors. They can send you a *multiple listing service* (*MLS*), which is a listing of potential properties with descriptions, zoning, pricing, and even aerial maps and satellite photographs of the property and surrounding area. An MLS is free for you; realtors are willing to incur the small expense of an MLS to possibly sell you what you're looking for. Don't feel bad; listing your home on the MLS is free as part of their membership, and their only other expense is a little research time. If they find something you're interested in, call them to take you there. If the property is what you're looking for, they get their commission for the "cost" of only an email and a trip to the property—not a bad rate of return for them. A commission on a new home could be 6% or more. That's $30,000 on a $500,000 home (unless you take my previous advice and negotiate their commission).

Enlisting Friends, Family, and Others

You need to enlist everyone you know to help you in this process. Tell your friends, family, and co-workers what you're looking for. Tell people at your church. Put up index cards at your community bulletin board, dry cleaners, and grocery stores. Get the word out. You never know when people might need cash suddenly and want to sell property they have been holding for investment, or someone wants to sell when a family member passes away. I hate to say it, but when people need an apartment in New York City, they don't call rental agents or look at the classified ads; they look at the obituaries first.

Enlisting the help of others works equally well for finding a piece of property and for locating a homebuilder. At this point, you're in the interviewing stage for both homebuilders and properties.

note If you have selected a homebuilder and are considering buying a piece of property, ask if he will walk through any potential property you're looking at. Your homebuilder can quickly recognize any difficulties or additional expenses that might be involved in building on that piece of property.

Summary

This chapter has explained the importance of finding out whether a property comes with the house or it's your responsibility to find it first. You learned about the long list of questions you must ask and the advantages and disadvantages you must consider before buying a piece of land. You also learned some tips for finding a piece of property and using realtors, friends, colleagues, and family to locate your new property.

With all this information, it should be just a matter of time before you find the right piece of property in the right location at the right price for you to begin building your dream home.

See "Additional Resources" on page 4 for details on how to download a free list of property interview questions.

8

Start Planning Your New Home

The first stage of the design process in building your new home is developing the house plans or blueprints. The term *blueprint* comes from the medium these drawings used to be copied on, white lines on navy blue paper. Today's blueprints, like most other documents, are black lines on a white background.

How to Find Home Plans You Really Like

By the time most people have decided to build their dream house, they usually have a good idea about what they want to build. First, you need to decide what architectural style home you want to build. There are many styles to choose from: Greek revival, Mission Santa Fe, high Victorian, California ranch, Cape Cod, French country, craftsman, and antebellum, to name a few.

The second step in developing blueprints for your new home is estimating the size or square feet you require for your lifestyle or the maximum square footage your budget will allow. You can work closely with your homebuilder on determining this estimate. After you tell your homebuilder how much you have to spend, he'll know how many square feet he can build for that budget— the dollars on the dirt.

You also need to develop a wish list of other design elements you want to build into your new home. These elements can include, for example, the number of bedrooms and bathrooms, the number of stalls in the garage, whether you have a formal living room and dining room or go with a great room. When you and your homebuilder have discussed these major elements, you can begin to search for or design the perfect plans for you.

Where to Find a Good Selection of New Home Plans

Most people who are building a new "custom" home don't think to start with an existing set of plans. They think they need to start the design process from scratch. It's much easier to start with an existing tested set of plans and change them to meet your tastes and design ideas. If you can find a set that comes close to what you want, you're way ahead in the design process. I know that looking for existing house plans when you want to build a custom home seems counterintuitive, but it gives you a much better starting point. It's easier to see what you're looking for when you have something to refer to already. If you do a good job of searching available house plans, there's a good chance you could find the house you want to build already designed for you. That will save you a lot of work, a lot of time, and a lot of money.

Find Plans on the Internet, in Books, and with Your Builder

Finding house plans is easier than ever. A ton of plan books with every imaginable plan are available as a great resource. Some books are specific to architectural styles or floor plan types (open, conventional, railroad), and some are tailored to specific square footage.

When I say a ton of books are available, I'm not exaggerating. If each book available at Amazon.com weighed only 1 pound, there would actually be a ton and a quarter. Currently more than 2,400 house plan books and 150 home design software packages are available at Amazon.com.

You can also find great plans from the Internet, designers, architects, and builders themselves, as you'll see in the following sections.

How to Get the Perfect Plan

Usually people think of going to an architect first when deciding to design a new house. In the past, most municipalities and planning departments had regulations that actually required an architect and/or engineer to sign a set of house plans before they could be approved. With today's computers and computer-aided design (CAD) systems, almost anyone can create a great house plan. As a result, many planning departments require only the engineering computations provided free by truss manufacturing companies, but some departments still require an architect, an engineer, or both to sign the plans. It pays to check with your municipality before developing your house plans. If you do purchase a set of house plans you find on the Internet, find out whether they were designed by an architect or engineer and whether they come with a signature and license number. Most of them do.

Hiring an architect can be expensive. When I counsel my clients, I ask them if what they want is really that unique and unusual. Most likely, they can find something close to what they're looking to build in books or on the Internet. If money isn't a concern, if your new home will cost more than $1,000,000, or your home design is truly unusual, hire an architect. Be prepared to budget for it; a good architect charges between $6,000 and $10,000 for a set of plans he already has and possibly more than $100,000 to design your home from scratch.

tip

As with deciding on other professionals, such as builders, realtors, lenders, and title agents, check out your architect before you sign with him or her. Follow the same procedures you used earlier: Ask for a reference list, visit their clients, look at their work, and ask for their hourly rate and an estimate of how much it will cost to design your home.

The Internet is by far my favorite way to locate just the right set of house plans. There are more plans than you can look at in your lifetime, and they're reasonably priced. You can order study or planning sets for under $100, and many providers customize their plans to meet your needs.

Preparing for this chapter, I typed "house plans" in a Google search. Google returned more than 39,400 matches, many of which had from 15,000 to 18,000 sets of plans. They were easy to search, too. Just select the style, number of bedrooms, number of garage stalls, and two-story or single level, and the websites return only the floor plans that meet your criteria. You can view the floor plans, elevations, renderings, and often photographs of the actual constructed home.

These sites also offer a variety of tools and support, including mortgage lenders, material suppliers, building calculators, and design tips and tools. Here are a few of the websites I looked at that might help you:

- *CoolHousePlans.com*   http://www.coolhouseplans.com
- *DreamHomeSource.com*   http://www.dreamhomesource.com
- *HousePlanGuys.com*   http://www.houseplanguys.com
- *HomePlans.com*   http://www.homeplans.com/welcome.asp

There are plenty more to choose from. Just Google them!

After you've decided which set of blueprints you want to build from or start with, you have several options for ordering them. You can purchase a single set of plans for as little as $450 to $950. You can order a *submission set*, which contains the five copies most municipalities require when you're submitting blueprints for a building permit. The advantage of submission sets is that they include everything most building departments require, they're ready to go, and most websites I reviewed make whatever changes your municipality requires at no extra charge.

Many websites offer you the opportunity to purchase reproducible plan sets for around $700 to $1,100. Some sites offer the actual CAD file for around $1,500. This way, you have the actual computer files in the format most designers require, so you can make whatever changes you want to the original files. Many plan sites also offer a materials list for around $75, and you can purchase full-reverse (readable) plans for an additional $100 per order, which can be produced in around three to five days. For more information, see "What Are Study Sets of Plans?" later in this chapter.

note Most municipalities require submitting five sets of blueprints (a submission set), including separate framing, plumbing, electrical, mechanical, roof truss, and plot plans printed on 24×36-inch white paper. Some building departments require other plans and documents, such as site grading and draining plans, truss engineering calculations, and 2003 IRC/2003 IECC minimum level of energy efficiency. If you're purchasing a set of house plans from the Internet, check with your local building department first to get a copy of its Residential Building Permit Submittal Checklist. Nearly every house plan website guarantees that it will provide everything you need and in the format your building department requires to get your building permit. Before you purchase a set of house plans online, be sure the company you're buying your plans from will work with you to format the plans according to your municipality's requirements.

Starting with an Existing Set of Plans

Getting back to the idea of modifying an existing plan, nearly all websites offer custom design services. They have design teams that can custom design your new home, or they can modify your first-choice home plan to become your dream home plan. You tell them what you'd like in your dream home, and they put those ideas on paper, starting from scratch or a predrawn blueprint. They'll even design your house plans if you send them drawings on scrap paper, Post-It notes, or dinner napkins.

The average cost to customize a plan is typically less than 1% of the building costs. Many charge up to the national average of 7% of the building costs, which translates to an average modification cost of $800 to $1,500 in addition to the cost of the reproducible blueprint. Also, most websites give you a free cost estimate on revisions to your home plans within five business days. They can also provide these other services:

- One-on-one design consultations
- Original custom designs
- Custom kitchen and bath design
- Barrier-free conversions for the physically disabled

For a custom design, you supply the following:

- Specific list of changes
- Revised floor plan sketch, if available
- State in which you're building
- Foundation type desired (slab, standard basement, and so forth)
- Exterior wall framing desired (2×4, 2×6, concrete block, or other)
- Your contact information

Custom designers then respond with an estimate within three to five days and the changes in about two to three weeks, depending on the complexity of the changes. They handle a variety of requests, from changing the wall framing or foundation type to increasing or decreasing room sizes or changing exterior finishes. They can also design completely custom plans.

What Are Study Sets of Plans?

The following sections cover blueprint definitions to help you understand your options when ordering plan sets from the Internet, books, a designer, or an architect.

Study Set or Planning Set

A *planning set* gives you a more detailed look at home plans than you can see on the Internet. It includes all available elevations and floor plans. It's shown to scale so that you can experiment with furniture placement and traffic patterns before buying the full set of blueprints. Usually, you can recoup your cost for a planning set by buying five or more sets (or a reproducible set) of blueprints for that home within 60 days from your planning set purchase.

Construction Plans

Construction plan blueprints often include everything you need to build your home and are detailed, clear, and concise. Each has been quality checked by professionals so that your plans are accurate and workable, and the good news is that they cost a fraction of the fee for custom-drawn house plans.

note Most blueprints you find on the Internet are designed by licensed architects who are members of the American Institute of Building Design (AIBD) or the Council of Publishing Home Designers (CPHD). Many plans are designed to meet one of the recognized North American building codes (the Uniform Building Code, the Standard Building Code, the Basic Building Code, or the National Building Code of Canada) in effect at the time and place they were drawn. You need to ask what building code was used before you purchase your plans.

The blueprints or construction plans for most home designs include the following elements:

- Exterior elevations show the front, rear, and sides of the home and include notes on exterior materials, details, and measurements.

- Roof details show slope and pitch as well as the location of dormers, gables, and other roof elements, including skylights. Details can be shown on the exterior elevation sheet or on a separate diagram.

- Foundation plans include drawings for a standard, daylight, or partial basement and/or a crawlspace, pole, pier, or slab foundation. All necessary notations and dimensions are included.

> **tip** Foundation options vary for each plan. If the home you want doesn't have the type of foundation you'd like, a generic foundation conversion diagram might be available or can be designed for you.

- Interior elevations show the specific details of cabinets (kitchen, bathroom, and utility room), fireplaces, built-in units, and other special interior features, depending on their nature and complexity.

- Detailed floor plans show the placement of interior walls and the dimensions of rooms, doors, windows, stairways, and so forth on each level of the home.

- Schematic electrical layouts show suggested locations for switches, fixtures, and outlets. These details can be shown on the detailed floor plans or on separate diagrams.

- Cross sections show details of the home as though it were cut in slices from the roof to the foundation. The cross sections specify the home's construction, insulation, flooring, and roofing details.

- General specifications (remember them from specs and selects?) provide general instructions and information on structure, excavating and grading, masonry and concrete, carpentry, thermal and moisture protection, and specifications about drywall, tile, flooring, glazing (windows), caulking, and sealants.

Reproducible Sets

Reproducible sets are required if you plan to make design changes to the plans. These sets consist of line drawings produced on erasable, reproducible paper (vellum) for the purpose of modification. When alterations are finished, working copies can be made from them.

Mirror-Reversed Plans

You can order *mirror-reversed plans* if you plan to build the home in the reverse of the illustrated floor plan. Because the lettering and dimensions on mirror-reversed plans are printed backward, I recommend that you order only one of these plans as a study set. You need the full-reverse plans with all the text printed correctly for your construction blueprint and permit sets.

Full-Reverse Plans

Some plans are available with a *full-reverse* option. Like mirror-reverse plans, these plans are used when building the home in the reverse of the illustrated floor plan. With a full-reverse plan, the lettering and dimensions on the blueprints are printed normally. These plans are required when submitting blueprints for your building permit and could take three to five days longer to order.

Material Lists

An itemized *material list* shows the quantity, type, and size of the basic materials needed to build your home from your specific house plan. This list is necessary for cost estimating and ordering materials.

FHA/VA Description of Materials

Your bank might need an *FHA/VA description* to secure a loan through the Federal Housing Administration (FHA) or the Department of Veterans Affairs (VA). This list specifies the minimum grade of building materials required to meet FHA or VA standards and provides descriptions of materials.

Line-Item Estimate

A comprehensive *line-item estimate* from the R.S. Means Company provides a detailed cost estimate on materials, installation, and more for the specific home plans you choose. This estimate is based on building costs in the area where you plan to build. In most cases, you must purchase the home plans and provide the ZIP code of your construction site to receive this service.

note The R.S. Means Company publishes comprehensive line-item estimating books that have become the industry standard for construction estimating. These books provide detailed cost estimating on materials and installation and are regionalized for your area. The estimates that design websites provide are specific to the home plans you choose and the area you're building in.

Three-Tier Cost Estimate

A *three-tier cost estimate* based on construction costs in your area tells you what it will cost you to build your plans on a (1) tight, (2) average, or (3) higher-end budget. You need to provide the ZIP code of your construction site to receive this service.

Generic How-To Diagrams

How-to diagrams show plumbing, wiring, solar heating, framing, and foundation conversion diagrams. These diagrams detail the basic tools and techniques needed to plumb, wire, install a solar-heating system, convert plans with 2×4-inch exterior walls to 2×6-inch walls (or vice versa), or adapt a plan for a basement, crawlspace, or slab foundation.

Downloadable Project Plans

Many project plans are available for immediate download after you've purchased them. Because *downloadable project plans* are delivered right to your desktop, you eliminate shipping charges and can get started on your project immediately. These plans are usually provided in a PDF file format, which can be opened with Adobe Acrobat Reader (free from www.adobe.com).

Making Changes to the Plans

I've explained how you can change, alter, add to, delete from, or create a completely custom set of home plans from house plan websites. The system is the same if you're working with a non-Internet company or architect. As I discussed earlier, the least expensive way to modify an existing plan or create a totally custom design is to hire a designer. An architect can cost from $10,000 to more than $100,000 to provide the same service.

If you're set on using an architect, however, you can go back to the Internet to find a discount architect. Guess what? You can at www.discountarchitect.com. As an example, DiscountArchitect.com charges between $1.50 and $3.00 per square foot of livable space to develop your custom house plans. You're encouraged to use the site's free estimates to determine your initial cost. These plans can also include a plot plan showing the house's location on the property and all sidewalks, driveways, and so forth (remember flatwork, concrete walks, patios, and driveways?) for an additional fee. The site even helps you design custom plans for a remodeling project.

How the Builder Determines What's Included in Your New Home

Your builder can be a great source of new home plans. That's what he does: builds houses from house plans. Many builders have hundreds of different house plans in their files that they've used in the past. If you choose a builder because of the type of homes he builds, ask to see what plans he has already built. Many builders work with you to develop house plans for you, and many even develop your custom house plans free. You only need to ask.

ARCHITECTURAL DESIGNERS

Many custom homebuilders use architectural designers to custom-design homes. Architectural designers are experienced draftsmen who work almost exclusively for homebuilders. They aren't necessarily licensed architects. Often, you can have a 6,000-square-foot, one-of-a-kind, custom home designed to fit on a particular lot for as little as $3,000 to $3,500. This price includes direct communication with the designer and even a visit to your lot to determine topography and lot characteristics.

Communicating with your homebuilder before buying anything on the Internet is important. Your homebuilder can tell you whether redrawing the plan because of requested changes is necessary or whether the purchased plan was too costly to build. Also, only your homebuilder can give you an accurate cost estimate of what your new home will cost to build. Internet prices are a good place to start, however, while researching your new home.

Tell the Homebuilder Your Quality; He'll Tell You the Size

Determining what size home you can get for the quality you want gets back to the importance of dollars on the dirt. The homebuilder you select already knows his costs for building a new home. He knows what it costs to build a two-story or a single-level house. He knows costs per square foot for a home with Formica countertops and a home with granite countertops. Each different level of quality assumes that same level of quality throughout the home. Even though this is a generalization, if you give your homebuilder an idea of the quality of home you want to build, he can tell you quickly how it's going to be designed and what quality of appointments will be installed throughout. By simply dividing your budget amount by his cost per square foot, your homebuilder can tell you how many square feet of that type home he can build for you.

If you're supplying your own land, your homebuilder also needs the lot size. Depending on the municipality's setback requirements (see the Note in this section), the allowable building area on your lot might require your new home to have two stories to accommodate the maximum square footage you can build on your budget.

note Setbacks are the distances from the front, rear, and sides of your property in which no structure can be built. These setback distances are required by your local municipality. When these distances are subtracted from your lot, the remaining area you're allowed to build in might be too small to accommodate the total square footage you want. In that case, you need to add another story.

Summary

In this chapter, you've learned how to find home plans you really like and determined the best place to start. You've also discovered the most efficient places to begin looking for the best selection of new home plans and seen the multiple types of plans, options, and flexibility available on the Internet.

And if that wasn't enough, you've learned how to develop the perfect house plan for you and save time and money by starting with an existing set of plans. You've seen the many different types of plans available to you, learned who to contact when you want to make changes to them, and reviewed how your homebuilder determines what's included in your new home and how big it will be. With this knowledge, you should feel confident that you can go from concept to blueprint in the fastest and least expensive manner possible.

See "Additional Resources" on page 4 for details on how to download free sample blueprints.

9

Know What's Included in the Base Price

To determine what's included in the base price, you need to know all the questions to ask before you can understand what the answers will be and what options are available. These options are called "specs and selects." Here's where the "home" work really begins. In this part of the project, you begin to collect all your ideas, preferences, styles, choices, and design elements that will go into your new home.

The best way to comprehend all the design decisions you need to make is to start by making a list. That's where the New Home Ideas Workbook comes in. To best understand how to answer each design question, do your field work by visiting model homes, showrooms, home warehouses, home and garden shows, and the Internet. To communicate all these design ideas to your homebuilder, you need to collect brochures, take photographs, print product information from the Internet, and get all these materials organized in a file.

Putting Together a New Home Ideas Kit

Your first "home" work assignment for this part of the book is to build your New Home Ideas Kit.

In this chapter:

* Work with the New Home Ideas Workbook

* Buy a custom home for the cost of a production home

* Make your home better by collecting your design ideas in advance

* Get organized to save yourself time, money, and mistakes

* Learn from other successful floor plans

This kit is applicable whether you're building a custom or semi-custom home or remodeling or adding on to an existing home. You need the following tools and supplies: a notepad and pencil, a 6-inch plastic ruler, a 12-foot tape measure, a marker, a digital camera, and an accordion file.

I've put together a New Home Ideas Workbook that you can download free after you register this book at Que Publishing's website (http://www.quepublishing.com/). Refer to this book's introduction for the details. Print out your workbook and look it over. The purpose of the workbook is to make you think about all the decisions you need to make when designing your new home. Before you begin building, complete this "fill in the blanks" workbook as best you can. When you're finished, you'll have a reference for your subcontractors, products, and warranty information that you can use if you ever have a problem after the home is yours. You can also use this information later if you decide to add on or make a change. You can even use this workbook for your homeowner's insurance because it has a space for costs, serial numbers, models, and dates of installation.

Here's an example of the New Home Ideas Workbook:

The New Home Ideas Workbook (Example)

Interior Rooms

Kitchen

Bathrooms

    Master Bathroom

    Bathroom #2

    Guest Bathroom

    Kid's Bathroom

Bedrooms

    Master Bedroom

    Bedroom #2

    Guest Bedroom

    Kid's Room #1

    Kid's Room #2

Great Room

Living Room

Formal Dinning Room

Home Office

Laundry

Interior Rooms

Storage Areas

Garage

Mechanicals

Patio/Deck

Foyer/Entryway

Exterior

Miscellaneous

Phone Numbers

Notes

Kitchen

Cabinets

Brand and Style:

Installed by:	Date:
Cost (if applicable):	Notes:

Countertops

Brand and Style:

Installed by:	Date:
Cost (if applicable):	Notes:

Appliances

Ranges, Cooktop

Brand and Model:

Size:	Height:	Width:	Depth:
Installed by:	Date:		
Cost (if applicable):	Notes:		

Refrigerator/Freezer

Brand and Model:

Size:	Height:	Width:	Depth:
Installed by:	Date:		
Cost (if applicable):	Notes:		

Microwave/Convection Oven

Brand and Model:

Size:	Height:	Width:	Depth:
Installed by:	Date:		
Cost (if applicable):	Notes:		

Interior Rooms

Faucet			
Brand and Model:			
Cost (if applicable):	Notes:		
Sink(s)			
Brand, Color, and Model:			
Installed by:	Date:		
Cost (if applicable):	Notes:		
Room Lighting			
Type#1	Type #2	Type #3	
Brand, Color, and Model:			
Quantity			
Installed by:	Date:		
Cost (if applicable):			
Notes:			
Replacement Bulb Types			
Type #1	Type #2	Type #3	
Part No./Model			

Next, go to your local stationery warehouse or office supply store and purchase an accordion file with built-in compartments or pockets that pull open so that you can file several items in one file. You often see smaller versions of accordion files used for collecting coupons. You're going to use this file to begin gathering your design ideas. After you have your accordion file, label the file compartments with logical headings from your workbook: kitchen, master bedroom, living room, garage, landscaping, or whatever.

Now you're ready to begin collecting design ideas and elements for your new home.

To do list

- ☐ Get cost estimates on everything.
- ☐ Negotiate.
- ☐ Prioritize.
- ☐ Select your hit list.
- ☐ Confirm these hit-list estimates with your homebuilder.
- ☐ Add the hit-list estimates to your agreement as addendums.

Getting Inspired by Model Homes

New subdivision model homes are a great way to ~~steal, plagiarize, borrow,~~ be inspired by new design ideas. The best of the best architects, planners, landscapers, and interior designers are hired to create award-wining model homes.

Remember the tape measure and digital camera I mentioned earlier? Now's the time to use them. When you go to model homes in your area, speak with the sales representatives, and get the floor plans and elevations for the models you like the best. Study them to see what you like about them and what you would do differently. Maybe the formal living room is too big for your lifestyle. Maybe the placement of the family room should be reversed with the living room. Maybe you'll fall in love with a window treatment, a floor style, a paint combination, a cornice molding.

This is where a digital camera comes in handy. Take a lot of pictures. Print them and organize them room by room in your accordion file. Keep the pictures organized in folders on your computer as a backup. When it's time to pick out design elements for each room, you'll have many samples of what works for you, and you can incorporate those samples into the design of your new home. By the way, if you like enough of a certain house's design elements, you might want to save some time and simply buy it! Don't rule that idea out.

Are You Getting What You Pay For?

When you walk into model homes with floor plans and price sheets in hand, how closely do you think the model matches the price sheet? In most cases, it's not even close. You can't blame the homebuilders because they fancy up the model homes to make them show better. It's similar to sprucing up your house when the in-laws come over for the holidays. Your home probably looks better than it does in the middle of a workweek.

You need to know exactly how wide the gap between appearance and cost is for both production and custom/semi-custom homes. This gap is where "standard options" come in. Spend some time with the homebuilder or sales reps and make sure you ask what the differences are, what's included, and what has been added to make the model show better. You'll be surprised at the differences.

note Standard options are discussed in more detail in Chapter 11,"What You Need to Know About Standard Options."

If you do decide to buy a particular production home and many of the model's features don't come with the home's base price, don't fret. You can talk to the homebuilder or sales reps to find out how much each upgrade costs. You learn how to have these negotiations and how to save money on these upgrades later in the book (see Chapter 11). Just be patient.

How You Confirm the Negotiated Price

Get what you can afford. Part of the process of doing your "home" work is getting prices for upgrades and add-ons. Remember: You have to pay for them as well with your original loan. When you're prequalified for a set amount, that's pretty much it. You have to keep your total construction costs lower than or equal to that number, especially if the monthly payment is based on your debt-to-income ratio. Toward the end of your project, if you begin running over budget and out of cash, putting those extras on credit cards adds significantly to your total monthly payments. You might have to decide to do without those upgrades for now, or you'd put your family and yourself under undue financial stress. There's no reason to do this. You can always add upgrades a year or more down the road.

When you take the time to investigate the cost of each upgrade, get multiple bids for negotiating the costs with your homebuilder, and prioritize your upgrades. You might be surprised by how many of those upgrades you can include in your new home project. For upgrades that don't make your hit list (list of first choices), keep the information in your file folder. Next year, you can give your spouse an upgrade for your anniversary or his or her birthday. You can always tear out carpet and have tile laid next year. Your floor isn't going anywhere, and you can certainly live with the standard carpet for a year or more.

After you have decided which upgrades to include in your design and what will be an add-on at a future date, commit the decisions in writing. Work with your homebuilder to include them in your specs and selects, or include the cost estimates as an addendum to your purchase agreement. This way, there are no misunderstandings at the time of closing. You and your homebuilder have agreed what will be done, what will not be done, and what the associated costs are, and this information is now part of your agreement.

Building Begins with the Specs and Selects

I'm going to talk about specs and selects a lot in this book because they're essential to the building process. "Specs and selects" is short for *specifications and selections*. Specifications are part of the blueprint package that specifies all the building details that go into your new home, such as 2×6-foot exterior walls, 12-foot ceilings, hollow-core doors, and R-32 insulation. Selects refer to the select sheets you fill out with your homebuilder that document your selections (from the accordion file) and list all your design choices. Your selects are usually picked from the homebuilder's list of standard options. Becoming familiar with the terminology during this early stage of design is important, even when you first start speaking with your homebuilder or designer. You can, of course, jump ahead and read Chapter 10, "Selects and the 5,000 Decisions Necessary to Build a New Home."

You Need to Communicate with Your Homebuilder

When you're working with a good homebuilder, you'll discover that he's always busy. It's just the nature of his business. He's coordinating 30 different subs on 10 different projects in 5 areas of town, working with 14 different homeowners, 8 different banks, 6 different realtors.... Don't ever assume that you and your house are all he has on his mind.

Did I mention that communication is the key? It is. When you get your homebuilder to sit down to discuss your needs and wants, document what you discussed and what changes you agreed to. Write a summary on a napkin or pad of paper, and then go home and type it in your word processor. It takes only a minute. Then fax it. This bears repeating: Fax it! Oh, yeah, *fax it!* Although your homebuilder might have good intentions, there's a good chance that between the time you speak with him and the time he gets back to his office where he logs changes into your binder, he'll have had 13 phone calls, 8 job site visits, and 15 problems to solve. He'll forget, and your home will be built without the change.

Faxing a document summarizing your request or conversation helps you and your homebuilder. It also helps guarantee that you'll get what you want because it's a good way to document what you and your homebuilder agreed to. In the worst-case scenario, this document might become important later if your requests weren't carried out and it comes down to who pays or who fixes the problem. Your lawyers need documentation of these agreements, and it helps to have a written statement of what was discussed and a verification that your homebuilder has a copy. Mostly, a fax document acts as a reminder to your homebuilder. With the many decisions you'll be making throughout construction, this documentation also serves as a reminder of what you agreed to with your homebuilder.

Don't Leave Money on the Table Because of Comps

In Chapter 5, "Building Your Team of Professionals," I mentioned "comps"—getting comparable values for similar houses in your area with similar square footage, number of bedrooms and baths, and so forth. Keep in mind that comps are only a starting point, however. This guideline holds true for new home prices as well. The amount you can negotiate varies considerably with the homebuilder, area, market conditions, and type of home. For example, if you're buying a production home, keep in mind that production homebuilders don't negotiate.

Comps Are Only a Starting Point

Comps are only a starting point. The true value of your existing home is what someone else is willing to pay. The only true cost for building your new home is what you're willing to pay.

To get a starting point for selling your existing home, your realtor runs your comps. To do this, she goes into the multiple listing service (MLS), and enters your lot size, square footage of your home, number of bedrooms and bathrooms, and so on. The report shows all the homes in your neighborhood that sold within the past year or so. Your realtor compares your home's square footage and other elements to the houses in your neighborhood that sold to determine an approximate beginning sale price for your home.

As I mentioned, this comp price is only a starting point. For example, in my neighborhood, all the homes are about 17 years old and most haven't been remodeled. A typical home in that neighborhood has mauve tile and carpet, Formica countertops, and brass and beveled glass light fixtures. Recently a realtor friend ran the comps on my home, and the price was about $100,000 less than what I expected for a home that had been completely remodeled recently. The discrepancy was difficult to figure out at first. It turned out that my home was, for all intents and purposes, brand-new, but the others that have sold over the past year were not. Each required between $50,000 and $100,000 for remodeling, which all the buyers did. This difference made the sale price and comps of other homes representative of the before-remodeling value. My home needed to be at the after-remodeling value. This type of inconsistency isn't necessarily reflected in the comps.

There are many reasons that one person would be willing to pay more (or less) for your home than another person. One of my homes sold for more because of its view, and another because it had a koi pond and a place for a grand piano. Two others sold at higher prices for a common reason: The buyers were moving from an area of the country with inflated real estate prices, which affected their perception of the value.

All these reasons apply to negotiating the price of your new home with your homebuilder. For example, your homebuilder might be willing to lower his price per square foot because he has a gap in his building schedule and would rather lower his price than lose a month or two of income. Your homebuilder might need immediate cash flow, so he's willing to trade an immediate deposit for a few dollars off his price per square foot. Your homebuilder might even be negotiating a huge loan with his financial institution and wants his financials to look their best. All these examples show why negotiation is to your advantage.

There are two areas where negotiating doesn't help much, but try it anyway. First, in a true seller's market (the supply is lower than the demand), you probably can't negotiate. When high-priced homes are selling quickly, there's not much room for negotiation. Second, negotiation is generally fruitless with production homes. These homes are usually priced at fair market value, and the margins are as tight as the homebuilder is willing to go. Also, production home prices are determined at corporate headquarters based on current and anticipated material costs, labor rates for that area, cost of that area's infrastructure (streets, parks, sewer, water, gas), the cost of the company's money (loans and interest), and often shareholders' dividends and the boards of directors.

Negotiating Can Save You More Than You Think

Custom and semi-custom homebuilders generally have smaller businesses to run than production homebuilders do. In addition, they don't have shareholders to worry about (except maybe a spouse) and can vary the cost per square foot more easily than production home companies can.

Negotation also depends on the homebuilder's current financial condition. If he needs your cash to finish the home he's currently working on, which happens frequently, he might be willing to lower the price and sign the contract so that you don't walk away. A bird in the hand, after all. You won't know, however, until you try. You have absolutely nothing to lose and everything to gain. If you can negotiate a $10-per-square-foot discount on a 3,000-square-foot house, you'll have saved $30,000 in construction costs! That's certainly worth trying.

caution Some homebuilders, especially small-scale ones, might have quoted you their rock-bottom price per square foot and just can't negotiate down. If you press them too hard, they might need to cut corners to try to make that profit back. Exercise good judgment when negotiating. You don't want to lose in the end.

WHY PRODUCTION HOMEBUILDERS TEND TO BE LARGE BUSINESSES

Most custom and semi-custom builders are mom-and-pop organizations. Although many of these businesses are large with 30 or more employees, most are small with fewer than 5. As a rule, production home companies are large. It takes a great deal of money and other resources to purchase a square mile of land, build a manufacturing facility, and construct anywhere from 300 to 6,000 new homes in one subdivision.

Production home companies are usually publicly traded corporations with CEOs and a board of directors that set the price per square foot scientifically with exacting margins based on hundreds of financial factors. A custom homebuilder, on the other hand, usually determines his cost per square foot by what it cost him to build his previous house.

Two examples of publicly traded production homebuilders are Kaufman and Broad (K&B) and Centex Homes, both considered among America's finest production homebuilders. In 2004, K&B built 31,646 new homes, generating revenues of $7.05 billion (http://www.kbhome.com). Centex Homes (Home Division) built 30,358 new homes, generating $7.60 billion in annual revenues (http://www.centex.com).

Production (Tract) Homes Can Produce Good Results

Production (tract) homes are usually a good value. If you can find one that meets most of your design criteria and fits your lifestyle, you might want to consider buying it. Production homes offer good quality and good value, and you can move in more quickly than you can into a custom/semi-custom home. Also, the infrastructure is usually in place already—schools, shopping, gas stations, and so on. You do need to compare production homes for cost, standard options, types of construction, quality, financing, and perks.

WHY PRODUCTION HOMES ARE CALLED "TRACT" HOMES

The word "tract" is often confused with "track." The term *tract home* refers to the tract, or large parcel, of land on which a community of production homes are built.

After World War II, tens of thousands of soldiers returned ready to get married and start their families (which eventually resulted in the baby boom) and needed affordable housing. In Long Island, New York, and later in Pennsylvania, William and Alfred Levitt pioneered a radical new design for community development called the "Levitt design." Both communities were called Levitttown.

The Levitt design provided an abundance of new, good-quality, low-cost housing. In 1952 the Levitt brothers built thousands of nearly identical 800-square-foot Cape Cod–style homes at an estimated cost of $5,000 each. This mass production of so many similar homes reduced the cost per home significantly.

The rectangular design and simple gable roof of the Cape Cod maximized the interior square footage while minimizing the more expensive exterior wall and roof construction costs. The simple kitchen addition at the rear of the home with a traditional shed roof resulted in what's called a "saltbox" architectural design. The saltbox design is cost efficient and was a popular architectural style during the 1700s.

Even if you decide at this point to buy a production home, you owe it to yourself to finish this book. Much of the tips, descriptions, and discussion throughout the rest of this book can help you through buying a production home every bit as much as building a custom or semi-custom home.

After you have checked out several production homebuilders and met and negotiated with several custom homebuilders, you might find that the prices are so close that a custom home is your best option. Also, a custom home usually commands a higher resale value because of the common perception that custom homes are built better and are more expensive to build. We'll keep the real cost just between us.

tip A lot of production home-builders have perks, such as a free $20,000 swimming pool for using their financing company. If you purchase before a given date, they give you a few points off your loan. As long as the rates are the same or better than you can find elsewhere, why not go with them? They might even offer a free upgrade or two. Sometimes there really is a free lunch—or pool, in this case. Do your "home" work, and don't be afraid to ask for free stuff.

If you're using a realtor to help with locating and comparing production and custom/semi-custom homebuilders, you must have your realtor with you when you register with sales agents at production home sales offices. If you don't, your realtor will *not* get paid a commission for helping you. Losing a commission certainly doesn't motivate your real estate professional. Remember, it's all about commission. That's the only way realtors get paid for all their work. Also, be aware that in a seller's market, many production homebuilders don't pay any sales commission or maybe only a flat $500 commission to your realtor. This reduced commission often discourages realtors from bringing clients to homebuilders.

Can You Buy a Custom Home for the Cost of Production?

I've mentioned being able to buy a custom/semi-custom home for the same price as a production home. When making comparisons, however, remember to compare apples to apples. Don't fall into the trap of setting your expectations high for a custom home. When you compare the costs, be sure you're not comparing a production home with solid-surface countertops and 8-foot ceilings to a custom home with granite countertops and 12-foot ceilings. These items are considered upgrades for production homebuilders, but for most custom homebuilders, they're standard options and are included in the base price. You need to compensate for those differences when comparing prices.

This comparison is similar to comparing prices on two new cars. You can't make a direct comparison between one with $10,000 spinner wheels, a 200-watt boom box stereo, and a custom paint job to one sitting in the showroom. However, you can make a comparison by adding the extra costs for the custom options.

When comparing production and custom/semi-custom homes, you also need to consider the land cost. With a production homebuilder, the land is almost always included; with a custom homebuilder, it might not be. Don't forget this factor.

How Is a Production Home Produced?

Production homes are designed and built from the ground up as inexpensively as possible while maintaining high standards of quality. Almost all production homes are actually manufactured in a factory on an assembly line. The manufacturing process is controlled precisely; the lumber meets exacting specifications, and computers mark and cut the pieces as they travel down a conveyor belt to a large table where pneumatic nail guns fire like machine guns.

The dimension lumber (2×4-inch or 2×6-inch are called *dimension lumber*) runs in continuous lengths connected end to end by finger joints that are stronger than the wood. As the dimension lumber moves down the conveyor belt, a computer-controlled circular saw darts across the belt, cutting the wood to the exact length. When the pieces arrive at the end of the belt, they are placed on large tables; assembled into wall, floor, or roof structures; labeled; and then sent on a flatbed truck to your new homebuilding site.

After the truck arrives at the site, framers quickly erect the house a section at a time until it's complete. From there, the process is similar to building a conventional home. Next comes the electrical work, plumbing, air-conditioning rough-ins, and so on.

This assembly-line process ensures that the materials are uniform, the workmanship is consistent, and the costs are minimized, which gives you, the homebuyer, the highest quality home at the lowest possible price. To review the pros and cons of production homes, please refer to Chapter 1, "Making the Decision on What to Build."

Make Your Home Better by Collecting Your Ideas in Advance

We talked about getting some awesome ideas from model homes, but model homes aren't the only place to look for great ideas, you can look for them in newspapers, home magazines, home centers, friends, neighbors, television, home and garden shows, and retail stores for plumbing and lighting fixtures, furniture, spas.

A File Can Save You Time, Money, and Mistakes

The accordion file I mentioned previously is a great for your home ideas because you can organize the partitions room by room. Here's another filing suggestion: Buy a plastic double-drawer filing cabinet with wheels from a local discount store for under $20. You can use this cabinet to keep your accordion file, realtor contracts, title company information, loan documents, floor plans and elevations, notes, and more. You can keep all the information you need for your new home in one organized safe place, and it's fun to roll around, too.

Brochures Can Communicate Your Ideas Better

While you're at home shows and home centers, grab brochures to take home. If you collect a brochure for every design element you want in your new home and store it in your accordion file, when it's time for your homebuilder to develop specs and subcontractor bids, there's little doubt about what you want.

Brochures are a helpful starting point for discussing what design elements you're thinking about. A pile of brochures showing what you want for your kitchen faucet, sink, countertops, cabinets, drawer pulls, and lighting gives your homebuilder a clear picture of your expectations. This information also helps him get exactly what you want, and makes it possible for him to warn you of potential additional costs for upgrades, which eliminates unpleasant surprises.

A Picture Is Worth a Thousand Dollars

Photographs are invaluable in conveying exactly what you want to see as design choices. If you want a particular type of coffered ceiling or a certain style of raised-panel kitchen cabinet, for example, you can simply hand your homebuilder a photograph and say, "I want this." There's no misunderstanding. Your homebuilder knows exactly what you're asking for. He can even show the photograph to his subcontractor when designing and pricing that part of the job, which can help prevent a lot of costly errors.

Aside from the cost of the camera and printing, taking pictures of your design elements is absolutely free. A picture really is worth a thousand words—*and* a thousand dollars. And a thousand pictures are worth… well, you do the math.

When you sit down with your homebuilder, designer, or architect, bring a copy of all your pictures for their records. This way, as they begin to develop designs for your new home, they can refer to the photographs often. Having photographs helps you get a draft design closer to what you want and can save you time and money.

Collecting Floor Plans Helps You Plan Better

Make sure you get floor plans. Floor plans and blueprints were discussed in Chapter 8, "Start Planning Your New Home," but I want to remind you to start collecting and filing them. Get the elevations, too. In case you're not familiar with the term, elevations are the part of the blueprint that shows views of the side, front, back, and roof of the house. They help considerably when designing the floor plans and basic layout of your new home.

SUCCESSFUL FLOOR PLANS GIVE YOU PROVEN DESIGNS

An occasional problem when building a fully custom home is that certain design elements just don't work. They work on paper but not in real life. You can't see what the house will look like until it's built, and then it's a little late if there's a mistake.

In my home, the second-floor bathroom was extended two feet to accommodate a larger tub. No problem, until I tell you that the bathroom floor extends over the entryway in a home with a 2 1/2–story vaulted ceiling. Room sizes, traffic-flow patterns, storage space, curb appeal, and scale are all factors in building your new custom home.

One advantage of using an existing house plan is that it has been tried and tested. With house plans that have been built before, any errors have been worked out already. In addition, they are less expensive, and construction can begin more quickly. An alternative is finding an existing house plan you like and modifying it to suit your tastes, lifestyle, and design choices. This option makes your new home plan the best of both worlds.

Summary

You have learned how to use the New Home Ideas Workbook to help organize all your design decisions and make sure you don't overlook anything. Getting inspired by model homes can also help you in the design process by building on the good ideas of others.

It's important to know whether you're getting what you pay for, know how to confirm the negotiated price, and know how to review specs and selects.

Communicating with your homebuilder helps ensure that you get the house you want and avoid errors. In addition, you learned not to leave money on the table because of comps and how you can save money by negotiating everything. You also saw how a production home is manufactured and how it's possible to buy a custom home for the cost of a production home.

Collecting your design ideas in advance and organizing them can save you time, money, and mistakes. With brochures, pictures, and floor plans, you can communicate your ideas more clearly.

You've covered a lot of material in one chapter, but this knowledge will help you make design decisions, communicate them to your builder efficiently, and negotiate the best price for each design element. Your homebuilder and other professionals make almost all the other decisions, but the process of design decisions is your biggest responsibility during the construction process. Now you're ready to take on the challenge.

10

Selects and the 5,000 Decisions Necessary to Build a New Home

It's estimated that approximately 5,000 separate decisions need to be made while building a new home. Luckily, the homebuilder makes many of them for you, and others are made based on previous choices. Selects are the major decisions you need to make.

This is by far one of the most important chapters you'll read in this book. Specs and selects (specifications and selections) are the number-one reason for cost overruns, errors, project delays, and lawsuits. They require the most planning, research, and documentation. The better you do with understanding, selecting, and communicating your specs and selects to your homebuilder, the more pleasant the building process will be and the closer your home will be to your dream. This chapter applies to custom, semi-custom, and production homes, renovations, and even remodeling.

Why Are Specs and Selects So Important?

All the previous chapters on doing research and filing ideas for your new home come to fruition in

In this chapter:

✳ Learn why specs and selects are so important to the construction of your new home

✳ Understand why making your selects on time can keep your project on schedule

✳ See an example of how to use your selection sheet

✳ Follow your builder's construction schedule to keep your participation and your project on track

✳ Learn how colorizing your selections makes your home more coordinated

✳ To download the free New Home Ideas workbook, sample select sheets, and a builder's schedule, see page 4

this chapter. The specs and selects process is where you communicate your wishes and desires for your new home to your homebuilder. During this process, he communicates what he can and can't do for the base price, what are considered upgrades, and what those upgrades will cost you. When you're done with this process, you'll know exactly the type and size of home, number of rooms and bathrooms, ceiling height, type of doors and windows, colors—the works.

What Are Specs and How Do They Affect Your New Home?

Specs are the design criteria that go into building your new home. They are developed by your builder and appear in two formats: as design elements included in blueprints of your new home or as an itemized list called the *building specs*. Specs determine items such as exterior wall thickness, ceiling heights, door dimensions, plumbing, insulation type, roofing materials, stucco, wiring gauges (sizes), construction of the concrete foundation, and type of exterior framing. Specs describe how the home is built and what it's built with.

Building specs are categorized by subcontractor. This way, when your homebuilder sends your house plans out to have his subcontractors develop their bid prices, each subcontractor gets a specific blueprint (plan) set and spec list. For example, electricians bidding on your home get a set of electrical blueprints and a copy of the electrical specs. Having this information assures your homebuilder that he can build your home for the price he quoted you.

This information tells the electrician everything he needs to know about what's expected during the course of construction: amperage, number of breakers, placement and number of receptacles (outlets), amount and size of wiring, light fixtures, and so on. This way, he can easily measure the feet of wire needed, count the number of light fixtures, and cost out the circuit breaker box, for example. If the specs are incorrect, the homebuilder will get an incorrect bid from subcontractors, so the electrician, for example, might not build that portion of your home correctly and to the homebuilder's and your specifications.

The specifications can include instructions on a customized feature you want, such as a meditation room on the roof, and might list how the homebuilder wants a certain subcontractor to follow a specific code. Specifications also state overall instructions, such as "All exterior walls shall be made of 2×6-inch spruce frame construction, free of material defect." Specs list everything a subcontractor needs to know to price and construct your home, including window types and sizes, interior and exterior doors, size and style of tiling, grout color and joint size, and more.

You, the buyer, must accept some responsibility for making sure these specs are correct and reflect your design ideas. To do this, make sure you read the finished specs before your homebuilder sends them to his subs, and discuss any specs that are incorrect or you don't understand. This task gets back to doing your "home" work and communicating with your homebuilder. Only after you and your homebuilder

have discussed, agreed on, and signed off on your new home's specifications should
he send the spec list out for bids.

What Are Selects?

Selects are your choices for optional design elements in your new home. After you
and your builder have reviewed his list of standard options (refer to Chapter 11,
"What You Need to Know About Standard Options"), you can get your accordion file
and go room by room, explaining exactly what you want in your new home.

Selects are all the visible design items you get to pick—carpet, tile, kitchen cabinets,
plumbing fixtures, light fixtures, door hardware, countertop materials, bathroom
hardware, and more. To see a sample of typical selects, check the free New Home
Ideas Workbook available for download from the web; see the introduction to this
book for details.

Making Your Selects on Time Can Keep Your Project on Schedule

Specs and selects are important for two reasons. First, you want your home built
your way. You don't want subcontractors or the homebuilder making assumptions
about what you want or having your great room painted periwinkle just because the
painter had a five-gallon can left over from his last job.

Second, you need to make these decisions in enough time for your homebuilder to
price them or send them to subcontractors for bidding. Perhaps most critical, you
have to make your selects in time for subcontractors to order materials and construct
that selection.

Here's a common example of the importance of making specs and selects on time:
At the beginning of a project, a homebuilder asks his homebuyers to pick out the
cabinets they want in their kitchen, hall, and bathrooms. They study several standard options the homebuilder or design center presents and discuss possible
upgrades with the homebuilder. The homebuilder tells the homebuyers that according to their construction schedule, he needs an answer on the cabinets by a specific
date. This date gives him enough time to first, have your cabinets manufactured,
and second, make sure the house has been built to the stage that the cabinets *can* be
installed.

Occasionally, with all the daily confusion the homebuilder and his office staff
deals with, he might forget to call and remind the homebuyers of their responsibility
to select their cabinet styles. The home continues under construction until the time
the cabinets need to be installed. Because many individual construction projects in
a new home depend on a previous project being completed, if the cabinets aren't
ready for installation, the projects grinds to a stop until they're ready. On average,
cabinets take 8 to 12 weeks for manufacturing. So in this example, home

construction could be shut down completely for up to three months while waiting for the cabinets to be built and installed.

To prevent this problem, work with your homebuilder by using his select sheet and construction schedule. Ask him to give you approximate dates for making each selection. Most custom homebuilders provide a schedule for you, and production homebuilders have their sales consultants or even an entire design center work with you on making your selections on time. Keep a paper or electronic calendar of your own. Mark the due dates for making each design selection and adhere to them. Nearly half of all homebuilding delays are caused by homebuyers. By following the schedule and making your selects on time, you can eliminate your half of the delays.

caution
Errors to Avoid   🛑 STOP

It's important to understand that delays can be expensive. If you're borrowing construction money from a financial institution or using the builder's construction money, there's an interest charge that continues while the home sits waiting for decisions. In addition, some homebuilders charge a monthly management or overhead fee, which can also get expensive if construction on your new home is idle. Be aware that after your construction scheduling is halted, resuming construction in a timely manner might be difficult. For example, if the framer is on another job, he could be tied up for weeks before he can return to your home. All these factors mean more costs for you and could result in major budget constraints.

Using the Select Sheet and Builder's Construction Schedule

As mentioned, more than 5,000 separate decisions and choices can go into building your new home, and some of those decisions are made in choosing selects. Ask your homebuilder to give you a *select sheet* and a *construction schedule*. The best time to discuss the select sheet and construction schedule is at the beginning of the project when you sign your agreement. Ask for those documents as part of your initial document package from your homebuilder.

These two documents help remind you what you need to decide and by what time. For example, the select sheet might list options for kitchen cabinets—wood type, finish, door style, and hardware style (if any)—and state that you need to give this information to your homebuilder on or before the end of the 16th week of construction. This way, the homebuilder can gather the information, send it to the cabinetmaker, and make sure he has enough time to construct the cabinets, schedule them for installation, and install them. The select sheet provides line items for all your design choices; the construction schedule tells you when in the project those decisions need to made. The construction schedule also helps you follow along with what's next and when the project is waiting for an inspection. Knowing when each decision is needed gives you the maximum amount of time for making decisions and helps keep you on schedule.

Using Your New Home Select Sheet

Making your selects on time is important. Delays in making selects can slow or stop the construction process and might also cost you more for rush orders, expedited shipping, overtime labor rates, and more. When discussing your selects, communicate your needs and desires to your homebuilder and do it on time.

Here's a sample of a homebuilder's select sheet:

> **tip**
>
> *Internet Information*
>
> If your homebuilder doesn't offer you a select sheet and construction schedule, ask for them. Communicate your desire to participate and help keep your project on schedule. If he still doesn't provide these documents, you can find samples of both in the New Home Ideas workbook. (The introduction to this book has details on how to download a copy of this workbook.) Although not every homebuilder builds at the same pace, the sample construction schedule is still helpful because scheduled tasks are in the same order for all homebuilding projects. You can simply adjust the timing to accommodate your project. Some homebuilders, especially production homebuilders, are reluctant to provide a construction schedule because they know the schedule will likely change. They don't want any potential legal consequences for not meeting the schedule they give you.

Sample Select Sheet

Front Door Selects

Style _____

Material _____

Finish _____

Upgrade _____

Order date _____

Interior Door Selects

Finish _____

Hollow core style _____

Upgrade: MDF solid core _____

Order date _____

Interior Closet Door Selects

Upgrade to mirror _____

Frame color _____ White_____ Chrome _____

Upgrade to beveled? _____

Garage Door Selects	
Style _____	
Model number _____	
Upgrade insulated? _____ White_____ Chrome _____	
Upgrade extra opener? _____	
Upgrade keypad? _____	
Order date _____	

This sample select sheet shows all the decisions for choosing just door styles. Although it might seem like a lot of work and look overwhelming, it's quite easy. You just answer the questions in order. To show you how easy it is, try walking through an example for the door selects, starting with the front door.

For the first question on style, your home-builder shows you pictures of available styles or directs you to his door supplier showroom, where you can select from the many different styles his distributor has to offer. So you decide on the style Tuscan #2270. For the second question on material, with the help of the door distributor, you decide on wood rather than insulated steel or fiberglass. For the question on finish, typical choices include painted, stained, or natural. You decide on walnut stain polyurethane gloss. Upgrades can include items such as additional weatherstripping and lites. For the last question, the order date, you can enter the date your homebuilder gives you from his construction schedule. Details such as dimensions, placement, and swing (which way the door opens from the outside) are included in your specs, on the construction schedule, and on your framing floor plan.

note In the door and window industry, the term "lites" refers to glass. If a door has a glass panel, it has a lite called a doorlite. If the lites are on the sides, they are called sidelites, and if they are over the door, they are called a transom lite (or just "transom"). With windows, you could have a "6 over 1" window, for example, which means six panes (or six divided lites) of glass in the top sash and one in the lower sash. For sliding-glass patio doors, you could call for an XO door, which means that looking at it from the outside, the panel of glass (or door) on the left is fixed (doesn't slide—denoted as *X*) and the panel on the right does slide (denoted as *O*).

Following Your Builder's Construction Schedule

The following construction schedule shows all the steps, permits, items to be ordered, and inspections. This information helps you follow along with the construction, be able to anticipate what happens next, know when your inspections are, and know when your selections need to be made. Here's a sample construction schedule:

Builder's Construction Schedule

Contract signed   Date_____

Start obtaining bids and contracts with subs   Date_____

File pre-lien notification builder's risk (if applicable)   Date_____

If septic, apply for permit   Date_____

Received permit   Date_____

Apply for construction permit   Date_____

Received permit   Date_____

Order water meter   Date_____

Order windows (confirm w/customer, verify color)   Date_____

Post all signs and permits on job site   Date_____

Important! Customer needs select sheet and needs to concentrate on plumbing (tubs, shower valves), roof tile if applicable, and exterior stucco color.

Important! Customer needs to set up account with local water company if not in subdivision. (Irrigated lots: Water to be scheduled by homebuilder during construction; however, lot owner responsible for invoices.)

Build pad for foundation   Date_____

Order engineering compaction test on pad   Date_____

Call for foundation layout and dig footings   Date_____

Order lumber and schedule framer   Date_____

Contact plumbing company for blue stake   Date_____

Set forms   Date_____

INSPECTION #1: Flood Control   Date_____

(Inspection: form elevations, plans needed on site)   Date_____

Rough-in plumbing and underground   Date_____

INSPECTION #2: Rough-in plumbing   Date_____

Grading and placement of steel (after inspection)   Date_____

Plumber to box and wrap after grading   Date_____

Electricians if plan calls for island or floor plugs   Date_____

Verify all windows with homebuyers and order   Date_____

Colorizing Is the Harmonizing of Your Decisions

Colorizing is selecting every item that goes into your new home and having them all complement one another. It also includes coordinating major architectural features, from doors, windows, and roofing materials to garage doors and exterior siding. Colorizing is as much about making sure the kitchen faucet works well with your architectural style as it is about coordinating the sink, cabinets, and drawer pulls. Colorizing is about matching a color in the tile with the color in the adjoining carpet. It's even about ceiling heights, wall textures, and wall coverings. Colorizing also includes making all these choices on time and on budget.

Now that you understand selects and specs and the all the decisions you need to make as you go through the homebuilding process, you need to know how to make those decisions so that they make sense together as a whole. As you go through the process of collecting and filing your ideas, photographs, and brochures for your New Home Ideas Workbook, keep in mind what all these choices will look like together.

When you fill in the description for each item and attach a brochure or photo, look at how the various choices work together. Ask yourself the following questions:

- Is it representative of the home's architectural style?
- What will this item look like next to other design choices in that room?
- Will it perform functionally to my expectations? (See the Note on this page.)
- Is it within my budget or should I consider it an upgrade?
- Most important, do I like it?

note The question of whether a choice will perform functionally to your expectations can apply to any item in your home. It can mean something as obvious as a kitchen faucet functioning as a handheld sprayer for filling pots or watering plants to stain-resistant wall paint and carpet if you have young children. It can also include more subtle functions, such as whether the color conveys the feeling you want in a room—a cool blue family room, a warm red bedroom, or a vibrant yellow breakfast area, for example.

After you have answered all the questions for that room or area, lay out all the brochures, photos, and samples of wallpaper, paint, tile, and carpet and see what they look like together. If you find them complementary and pleasing, then they're colorized.

Help with Interior Design Is Available

Interior design is one aspect of residential building that I've chosen to remain clueless about. I'm a left-brain kind of guy, and the whole color-wheel/pattern/texture/palette thing simply eludes me. That's the first step in interior design: knowing you might need a little help. If you're not comfortable with picking out all the design elements that go into your new home, you can always hire an interior designer. The purpose of an interior designer is to help you plan, design, and furnish interior spaces of your new home. He or she assists you by designing practical, aesthetic rooms that are conducive to your intended purposes and lifestyle.

Most people don't realize that the distinction between "interior designer" and "interior decorator." In many states, interior designers must have specialized training and a license just as real estate agents do before they can practice their trade. Designers are also trained to manage and supervise more complex projects that might involve subcontractors and complicated scheduling. More specifically, your interior designer might do the following:

- Estimate material requirements and costs and present designs for your approval.
- Confer with you to determine factors affecting the planning of interior environments, such as budget, architectural preferences, and intended function of the room.
- Advise you on interior design factors, such as space planning, layout, utilization of furnishings, and color coordination.
- Select, design, and purchase furnishings, artwork, and other accessories.
- Subcontract fabrication, installation, and arrangement of carpeting, fixtures, accessories, draperies, paint, wall coverings, artwork, furniture, and other related items.
- Render design ideas in the form of paste-ups or drawings.

The cost of an interior designer can vary widely from very reasonable to absurd, so you need to meet with a few designers and discuss their method of design, their experience, and how they bill. You can pay for an interior designer's services in several ways. Designers charge with a variety of fee structures and, as with other professions, base their fees on variables such as complexity of the project, its geographical location, and their expertise. Most designers use one of the following fee structures or combine them to suit your particular needs:

- *Fixed or flat fee*   The designer specifies a sum to cover costs, exclusive of reimbursement for expenses. One total fee applies to the complete range of services, from conceptual development through layouts, specifications, and final installation.
- *Hourly fee*   Compensation is based on the actual time the designer spends on your project or specific service.
- *Percentage fee*   Compensation is computed as a percentage of your overall construction project costs.
- *Cost plus*   The designer purchases materials, furnishings, and services (such as carpentry, upholstery, drapery, cabinetry, and picture framing) at cost and sells it to you at her cost plus a specified percentage you have agreed on.

- *Retail* The designer sells furnishings, fabrics, wall coverings, and all other goods to you at retail rates to cover her designer's fee and services. This fee structure is more applicable to retail establishments offering design services.

- *Per square foot* The designer charges fees based on the square footage of your new home.

A typical hourly fee for a well-known interior designer in your area might range from $75 per hour for a design assistant to $250+ per hour for a grand master, with $150 to $200 as an average hourly fee range.

In addition to the fee structures listed previously, designers might require a retainer before beginning a design project. A *retainer* is an amount of money you, the client, pays to the designer that's applied to the balance due at the completion of your project. The retainer is customarily paid upon signing the contractual agreement in advance of the design services and is not reimbursable. Retainers can run from $500 up to $1,200 per major room or about $5,000 to $10,000 for a typical three-bedroom home.

The method for finding an interior designer is similar to the process for finding all the professionals you enlist to design and build your new home. Start with referrals from friends, co-workers, and family, and check with local trade associations. Visit a few design studios (centers) and ask who they respect and can recommend. Design centers work with interior designers all the time and know who is good and who isn't, who is easy to work with, who is reasonably priced, and who is the best designer for your specific tastes and ideas.

You can also visit the American Society of Interior Designers (ASID) at http://www.asid.org, which maintains a database of thousands of professionals across the country. You can call the free referral service at 800-775-ASID and describe your project and budget, and the service gives you the names of three or more designers in your area. You can also use ASID's online referral service.

Keep in mind when you work with an interior designer, it's about what you like, not what your decorator likes.

SHOULD YOU HIRE AN INTERIOR DECORATOR OR DESIGNER?

In most cases, hiring a decorator or designer isn't necessary. Only about 25% to 30% of homebuyers work with a designer. Most homebuilders have someone on staff and contact people (preferred salespeople) with suppliers to help homebuyers with their selections. For example, a trained carpet salesperson usually has interior decorating experience and knows how to coordinate flooring with wall colors, cabinets, and so on. Kitchen and bathroom designers with cabinet suppliers are excellent at coordinating cabinet layout and style with your home's architectural style. They can also coordinate cabinet color and other wood choices with countertops, backsplashes, floor tile, wall colors, and hardware.

Hiring an interior designer can be worthwhile or occasionally disastrous. Many designers are inexperienced in new home construction, which can cause delays, budget overruns, interference with the construction process, and even conflict with the homebuilder, suppliers, and subcontractors. In one instance, a home-builder worked with a decorator who demanded hours of his time examining and pricing outlandish options, which ended up completely outside the budget. Other designers might insist on providing costs to the homebuyer instead of submitting them to the homebuilder and even try to hire their own sub-contractors.

You need to be aware of some of these issues and know that the designer is more like the homebuilder's subcontractor if she's used during the construction process. The homebuilder is still in charge of the overall project.

Summary

This chapter has emphasized why specs and selects are so important in the construction of your new home. You did your "home" work in previous chapters by gathering information you need to make design choices for your new home, and now you've seen how to commit these decisions on a select sheet.

You also saw how making your selects on time can keep your project on schedule and learned how to follow your homebuilder's construction schedule to keep your participation on track. This chapter also provided examples of a select sheet and construction schedule.

Last, it's time to be sure all the selects are colorized and match your other selections. When you're happy with your selections and colorizing, record those decisions and communicate them to your homebuilder.

See "Additional Resources" on page 4 for details on how to download a free New Home Ideas workbook, select sheets, and a builder's schedule.

Part III

Starting the Design Process

What You Need to Know About Standard Options

A s the homebuyer, you need to take the responsibility to discuss and understand what your choices are and what standard options are available with your new home. Understanding standard options helps you maximize your design choices while minimizing charges for upgrades and change orders. This knowledge can save you a lot of money and aggravation during the course of construction and result in a better home in the end. When you sign a contract with your homebuilder, don't take any standard options for granted. The contract should clearly spell out what the homebuilder is providing as a standard option and what you're paying extra for as an upgrade.

In this chapter:

* Learn what a standard option is

* Discover what your choices are and look at a list to give you some ideas

* Understand that if it's not standard, it's an upgrade

* Find out whether you can use your own sub-contractors

* Make your homebuilder's standard options part of your specs and selects

What Is a Standard Option?

When I was introduced to the term "standard option," I thought it was an oxymoron. If it's an option, how can it also be standard? A *standard option* is any choice the homebuilder offers to you; standard options are usually presented in a list of products that are standard design elements for the quoted price of construction. Anything that isn't part of the list of standard options is an upgrade.

You need to ask your homebuilder to show you samples and request a "spec sheet" that clearly lists standard and upgrade options.

Any time you go into a homebuilder's office, whether it's a custom or production homebuilder, you'll see a room that looks like an explosion at a home warehouse store. The kitchen cabinet doors, carpet pieces, floor tiles, faucets, vinyl floor swatches, and roof tiles that you see everywhere are the color samples and choices you can pick from for your new home's base price. Homebuilders with large companies often have *design centers* where you can sit down with a designer who assists you in putting it all together. These designers are also there to "upsell" you on upgrades, so be aware.

Know Your Choices

When you discuss standard options with your homebuilder, ask him about the following common new home features. Find out whether they are standard options or upgrades. If they are upgrades, how much will they cost you?

Inside Your Home

The following are some inside features of your home:

- *Windows (including bay, accent, and transom windows)*—Quality, type of glazing, low-E coating, material, cladding, and type of locks

- *Trim (around windows, doors, baseboards, and cornice or crown)*—Plain or colonial; natural wood, polyethylene, or MDF (see the Note in this section); natural or primed

> **note** Medium-density fiberboard (*MDF*) is a lightweight engineered wood product that cuts and works just like wood but with less movement (expansion and contraction) caused by changes in humidity and temperature. MDF molding comes primed and ready to paint.

- *Paint (interior and exterior)*—Type, quality, and colors

- *Patio doors*—Width, quality, type of glazing, low-E coating, and material

- *Carpet and underpadding*—Quality, material, weight, backing, rating, and manufacturer's warranty

- *Vinyl flooring*—Quality, colors, and patterns (see the sidebar "Linoleum Flooring")

LINOLEUM FLOORING

Linoleum is the term often used incorrectly to describe resilient floors made of vinyl. Linoleum was one of the first resilient floors, introduced in the 1800s. Made of linseed oil, gums, cork, or wood dust and pigments, linoleum is no longer manufactured in the United States.

- *Ceramic tiles (floor and walls)*—In bathrooms, kitchen, and entryway; includes colors, patterns, and finish (for example, nonskid)
- *Kitchen cabinets and bathroom vanities*—Type of materials, countertops, drawer pulls, pot drawers, lazy Susans, wine rack, microwave oven shelf, sinks and faucets
- *Bathroom fixtures*—Colors and quality; choices for pedestal sinks, vanity mirrors, shower stalls, Roman tubs, and whirlpool tubs
- *Bathroom hardware*—Towel bar, hand towel holder, soap dish, robe hook, toilet paper dispenser, and so on; includes quality, material, and color
- *Electrical fixtures*—Lights (interior and exterior), placement and type, receptacles and switches (standard or designer)
- *Appliances*—Type, quality, and color
- *Fireplaces*—Number, location, type, doors, trim, and hearth
- *Staircases*—Number; type; design of spindles, handrails, and risers; material, and finish

Outside Your Home

The following are some features of the outside of your home:

- *Cladding*—Brick, two-tone brick, cornerstones, stucco, imitation rock, other finishes
- *Porch and patio*—Size, material, and finish
- *Decorative design elements*—Shutters, trim, corbels, scuppers, bump-outs, other
- *Driveway and walkways (nonfoundation flatwork)*—Gravel, paving, interlocking brick, other
- Landscaping—Trees: type, number, and size; bushes: type, number, and size; sod in front and back; decorative stone, gravel, and decomposed granite; planter beds: number and size
- *Exterior lights*—Number, type, and quality

- *House numbers*—Location, style, and quality
- *Mailbox*—Size, location, and quality
- *Kickplates (for doors)*—Number, locations, and type

Your homebuilder wants you to be happy with your new home. Eliminate surprises and disappointments; sit down with your builder and discuss this list in detail. Add other items as you think of them. Know what you are getting for your money; that way you can make wise buying decisions that will provide you with satisfaction and peace of mind for a long time.

If It's Not Standard, It's an Upgrade

The importance of doing your "home" work is to prevent surprises or disappointments. Remember, anything that's not selected from your homebuilder's list of standard options is considered an upgrade. Depending on the item, this can mean it's a special order, requires extra deposits, takes more time to be delivered, or must have a subcontractor scheduled for installation (which always has an extra charge associated). The additional charge might be nominal or not. You need to identify any non-standard options you want in your new home and get an estimate of labor and materials charges from your homebuilder.

Can You Use Your Own Subcontractors?

Many homebuyers think a homebuilder won't allow them to do wiring themselves, have their Uncle Freddie do it, or hire their own subcontractor because they want to make the profit from that subcontractor. That's only partially true, but it's not the main reason.

In the United States, most homebuilders warranty the completed home for two years from the date of closing. That's a full year beyond the manufacturers' warranties on appliances and other equipment in the home. In some states, the law requires that a homebuilder provide a warranty on all new homes that guarantees the standards for construction and quality of the homes' structural elements and components. In many states, laws require a homebuilder to register with the state before starting construction on any new home. The law and regulations provide a limited 10-year warranty coverage against defects of materials, workmanship, and systems in a new home.

With these strict laws and regulations, no matter what happens in or around your new home, the homebuilder is responsible for correcting or fixing the problem for at least two years. So if Uncle Freddie installs some plumbing and it leaks or installs surround sound and it stops working, the homebuilder is responsible for repairing the problem for two years.

The consequence to the homebuilder can go even further. If someone added wiring over the weekend, for example, that resulted in a fire, the homebuilder would be responsible for the losses. In addition to monetary losses, the homebuilder could lose his license and liability insurance and suffer other legal consequences.

In one instance I experienced, the homebuyer did in fact hire someone to install electrical wiring over the weekend in what was originally to be an unfinished basement. The homebuyer assured the homebuilder that the person installing the wiring was a licensed electrician and a personal friend.

On Monday morning, the regular electrician reported to the job site to complete his wiring when he noticed the wiring done over the weekend. He discovered that it was poorly, illegally, and dangerously installed. The electrician walked off the job, demanding that all the wiring be ripped out before he returned. The homeowner refused to rip out the wiring because he had paid the other electrician (who turned out to be unlicensed) a large sum of money. The scheduled electrician explained to me that when he signs off on the home being complete, it's his license and liability insurance that protects the home. The homeowner insisted that the builder hire a third electrician to complete the home, which the homebuilder did.

When the home was complete and awaiting its final inspection from the town to secure its certificate of occupancy (C of O), the town refused. Somewhere along the line, the town heard what had happened (most likely from the scheduled electrician) and insisted that before issuing the Cof O, all wiring in the now-finished basement would have to be removed. This delayed the homeowner from moving in for close to a month and cost him a considerable amount of money to demolish the basement walls and ceilings and remove all the wiring.

If you want to do *any* work on the home yourself, your homebuilder must approve that work in writing. Most homebuilders will work with you on small projects that can save you money; this way, your homebuilder assume the legal responsibility for your work after the home is complete.

Make Every Standard Option and Upgrade Part of Your Specs and Selects

Discuss your homebuilder's list of standard options with him and make them part of your specs and selects. You also should make any design elements you want included in your home that aren't part of your builder's standard options part of the specs and selects after you've discussed these with your builder, as discussed in the previous section. Follow these steps:

1. Do your homework in selecting all the design elements you want built into your new home.

2. Understand your choices of standard options.

3. Determine which design elements you want that aren't on the builder's list of standard options.

4. Discuss those additional items with your builder and have him give you a cost estimate on labor and materials.

5. Have all the standard options and nonstandard options or upgrades added to your select sheet and specifications for your new home.

6. Have the builder sign off on the specs and selects.

Summary

In this chapter, you learned about standard options and the importance of knowing what your choices are. A sample list of standard options was provided to give you some ideas. You also reviewed the importance of specs and selects in your home-building project.

Remember: If it's not standard, it's an upgrade. Upgrades can be expensive and can slow down the project if they're not planned for in advance. Keep in mind, too, that using your own subcontractors can be hazardous to your homebuilding project.

12

The Benefits of a Builder's Allowance

Many decisions that go into the design and construction of your new home are a matter of taste, and as they say, to each his or her own. For this reason, most homebuilders prefer not to get in the middle of those decisions, as they don't materially affect the construction of your new home. As a result, most homebuilders give you a budget and a supplier where you can go and purchase whatever your heart desires (within budget). This way, your homebuilder simply installs your choices. Allowances are just easier for everyone.

Why a Cash Allowance Can Be a Good Thing

A *cash allowance* is a sum of money set aside in the construction contract for items that you haven't selected yet or that haven't been specified in the contract. These items don't affect the early stages of construction. An allowance is essentially a mini-budget for items you haven't decided on yet so that you can pick them out later.

In this chapter:

* Learn what a cash allowance is and why it can be a good thing

* Understand how a cash allowance works for you

* Find out how who pays the overage and who keeps the difference

Homebuilders usually offer cash allowances for three reasons:

- First, homebuilders don't want to get involved in your personal design choices, nor do they need to.
- Second, many of your selects have no bearing on the construction of your new home; they simply get installed.
- Third, it's easier for the homebuilder and you at the time of signing the contract. An allowance provides a budget or placeholder where your selects are included, but you don't have to make all your select choices before your sign your contract.

Many homebuilders, from custom to production, give you a budgeted amount for each category of selects that might include plumbing fixtures, electrical fixtures, carpet and tile choices, kitchen cabinets, and others. Your homebuilder also gives you a list of exactly what you need and a list of his approved suppliers with whom he has prenegotiated prices and charge accounts. It's then up to you to go to those suppliers and select everything you need. Cash allowances work for you because you control the quality, cost, and design.

A cash allowance acts as a placeholder in your contract that represents a sum of money dedicated toward an undecided aspect of the job. When you sign the contract to begin construction of your new home, most likely all the items haven't been decided. At that point, it's too early in the process for you to know all your choices. So the homebuilder places an allowance in the contract telling you that you have been allotted a certain amount of money toward the expense of that undecided selection.

Allowances help you see the true cost of your new home project, they keep you from having to remember to set aside money later for certain items, they commit your homebuilder to agreed-on budget amounts, and they make it possible to begin your new home construction without being forced to decide on every detail beforehand.

caution Keep in mind that the more allowances included in a contract, the more the final price exceeds the budget. This isn't because the allowance amounts are inadequate but because there are too many tempting options for homeowners today. You might have a tendency to want more (and a higher quality) of everything when you start the shopping process. So if you have a tight budget, letting the homebuilder make some of your selections and provide fewer allowances can be better. For example, your homebuilder might include certain GE Profile appliances in your contract instead of giving you an applicance allowance. Some shrewd homebuilders might include lots of allowances in every imaginable category knowing that you'll exceed these amounts, which can translate to more profit for the homebuilder.

Your homebuilder has probably built many similar homes during his career and because of his experience, knows the average cost of almost every item in a new home. He designs his cash allowances to be realistic and cover the costs for all items you need to complete your new home.

The following table lists some examples of common cash allowance items homebuilders provide and average dollar amounts for each item.

Typical Cash Allowances for an Average New House ($267,400)

Item	Average Amount
Cabinets	$12,000
Countertops	$3,000
Light fixtures	$3,000
Appliances	$4,000
Tile	$5,000
Hardwood flooring	$5,000
Vinyl flooring	$1,000
Carpet	$5,000
Landscaping	$10,000
Swimming pool	$20,000

Other lump sum allowance items can include wallpaper, door hardware, plumbing fixtures, shower doors, mirrors, closet shelving, block fences, and irrigation.

tip Of course, the numbers in this table will vary depending on your homebuilder, the quality of the home you're building, the square footage, the style of home, and the area of the country where your new home is being constructed.

Who Pays When You Exceed Your Allowance and Who Keeps the Difference?

If you spend over your allowance, you are issued a change order to authorize those purchases, and ultimately you're billed for the difference between your authorized allowance and what you actually spent. This agreement gives you, the homebuyer, an incentive to stick to a predetermined allowance for those items or at least forces you carefully consider deciding to go over budget on certain items.

When your selections are made and the supplier sends the invoice to your home-builder, your homebuilder *can* credit any amount under the allowance to you. I say "can" because some homebuilders credit that amount, but many homebuilders just don't issue credits back to homebuyers on allowances. They keep the difference. They provide the budget on those items, and that's what you can spend. Use it or lose it. So you need to ask your homebuilder before signing a contract "If I don't spend an allotted allowance, will the difference be credited back to me?" Asking that question up front could add up to a lot of money.

Be aware that low cash allowance quotes from your homebuilder could make the square-footage cost of your new home seem low at the start and encourage you to choose that homebuilder based on price. Later in the project, these unrealistic allowance amounts can increase the cost of change orders and upgrade costs after your contract has been signed and construction has already begun. The home-builder might quote you a cost of $128 per square foot and tell you that you have allowances for certain items, such as electrical fixtures. You might find out later that the allowance is far less than what you need to purchase all the fixtures. When you go over the allowed amount, the homebuilder then charges you extra for that over-age, which could drive the square-footage cost up another $2. If this happens on, say, five allowance categories, the actual cost per square foot could be $10 more. You need to ask and understand what your allowances are before you sign your contract.

Summary

In this chapter, you have learned that a cash allowance helps protect you at the time of contract signing by guaranteeing you have an agreed-on budget for items you're deciding on and purchasing later in the project. Understanding your allowances makes it possible to better define your actual square-footage cost. The issue of who pays the overage and who keeps the difference was also discussed.

Managing your cash allowances carefully can result in a large cost savings and get-ting the design elements you want. Working with your homebuilder and agreeing to realistic allowance budgets for each category is the first step. Managing those budg-ets and not overspending is the second step. If you follow these two steps, you can save a great deal on change orders and overages—and don't forget to ask your homebuilder who keeps any underages!

Get Your Own Costs and Compare

13

During the course of construction of your new home, you'll be asking for upgrades or other work that wasn't anticipated in the original agreement with your homebuilder. You and your homebuilder should discuss these changes or add-ons, and then he gives you a price for this work or refers you to one of his trusted subcontractors for a bid price. Getting your own costs is the only way you can know whether the price your homebuilder or subcontractor is quoting is a fair price.

In this chapter:

* Learn how to get your own bids to understand true costs

* Learn how to compare bids

* Learn how to use your specs to get accurate bids

* Learn how to minimize the financial impact of a bid error

To do list

1. Make an 8.5×11-inch copy of your floor plan or elevation that covers the area in question. (Copy your specs, if applicable.)

2. Find contact information for at least three (sub) contractors to perform the work.

3. Call all three to ask them to bid and get their fax numbers.

4. Fax them a copy of the plan or specs showing what you want.

5. Receive all the bids and compare.

When You Compare, You Know the Facts

When building your new home, there will be upgrades and other additions that your homebuilder doesn't want to do, such as landscaping, a block fence, or a swimming pool. Or he might charge extra for these upgrades and add-ons, such as additional tile, crown moldings, and built-in cabinetry. For these items, you need to learn how to get your own construction bids and check them against your homebuilder's prices. It might sound a little scary, but it's easy. Review the To Do list at the beginning of this section to get started.

Take the time to send out bids to at least three (sub) contractors, even if you have decided to pay your homebuilder to do the upgrade. In class, I ask students, "If you get a price from your homebuilder for $1,800 to tile an entryway, is that a good price?" About half say "No, the homebuilder is taking advantage of me," and the other half say "I guess that price sounds fair." Usually a few students admit they just don't know.

I then ask them, "How long is a piece of string?" After several moments, I tell them there's not enough information to answer either question. So the correct answer to the original question is that they don't know what a fair price is. If you agree with your homebuilder that the area to be tiled is 500 square feet and you want an inlaid medallion surrounded by imported 18×18-inch Italian marble, that's a good price. If you ask for only a

note In this chapter, I use the term "(sub) contractor" because when you hire someone to build a swimming pool or block fence, he might be a subcontractor, as for tile or plumbing who works for your homebuilder, or a general contractor working directly for you, as with a swimming pool company. The more specific the project is, the more likely that he does only that one task and nothing more. If the project is more complex, such as a swimming pool, the person you hire will most likely be a general contractor specializing in swimming pool construction. A swimming pool requires many different trades, such as excavation, ironwork (rebar), concrete, plumbing, electrical, gas or solar heating, plastering, tile work, decking, and maybe even landscaping, which the pool company might subcontract itself.

10×10-foot area tiled in a home warehouse ceramic tile, the price would be high. You just don't know what a fair price is until you do some "home" work.

How to Get Bids to Better Understand Your Costs

The process of finding (sub) contractors to ask for bids is similar to the process of finding your homebuilder. If you will most likely use your homebuilder for the project and are simply checking his prices, the whole due diligence process isn't necessary, unless he bids the upgrade too high and you decide to go with a (sub) contractor. If you're looking to hire a (sub) contractor, get the bids first, and then do your due diligence on the bidder you choose.

note A *tile medallion* is a complex picture made from tiny pieces of tile, often resembling a mosaic. These medallions are premanufactured and glued to a web backing. The outline of the medallion is tiled, and the medallion is then set into that outline and grouted into the surrounding tile to form a complex inlaid design. Medallions can cost from $150 for a simple design to well over $3,000 plus the installation cost. These patterns are often in the shape of the four compass points, a Greek scallop border, rectangular borders, and abstract geometric designs.

There are a lot of places to look for (sub) contractors to bid on your home project. You can look in the yellow pages under a specific trade, such as tile, landscaping, and swimming pools. You can also use television ads, home magazines, and newspaper ads. Take a look around. Many building companies offer specials, perks, and discounts, especially in their slow season. You can get great deals on swimming pool construction in January, for example.

Another place I go for most personal and business phone numbers is Switchboard (http://www.Switchboard.com). It's easy to use and always up to date. Just type in the category or company name, enter your city and state, and select the surrounding area, and in an instant, Switchboard displays a list, starting with the company closest to your home and moving farther out as you go down the list. It lists every company type you asked for, even 150 miles from your home. Switchboard also shows addresses, phone numbers, and often fax numbers. You can even click and get a map and directions to the company's office. Switchboard also offers a free screening service called ServiceMaster to help you select a company.

If your homebuilder isn't interested in building your project, he can give you contact information for some (sub) contractors who do that type of work for his clients. These (sub) contractors are people he has a relationship with and trusts, so they are a good first choice. Using a (sub) contractor with a personal reference, especially from your homebuilder, is always a good idea. If your homebuilder doesn't have a reference for the type of (sub) contractor you're looking for, ask one of this subcontractors. For example, ask your homebuilder's concrete or excavating subcontractors for a swimming pool reference. In many cases, they have been hired by a swimming pool contractor to excavate or pour concrete. They know who does good work, has fair prices, and pays on time. (Remember the litmus test of a homebuilder's financial stability from Chapter 6, "Doing Your 'Home' Work on Your Homebuilder"?)

Comparing Your Bids

When you get all your bids back, take the time to compare them. Make sure they all contain the same line items. Look for line items missing from a bid, look for items included that you didn't think of, and look for unnecessary charges. What you'll find is that the bids are very similar, and in most cases, you'll see that they turn out to have very similar totals. If one bid is way out in left field, and it's a lot lower or higher than the rest, it's probably wrong.

Generally, if you receive five bids back on a job, three are very close to one another, one is low, and one is high. The three in the middle are the true street price and are fair. These (sub) contractors took the time to read the request and respond accurately. The low bidder made a mistake, left something out of the bid, or bid low on purpose. Some less scrupulous (sub) contractors bid low deliberately to make sure they get the job. Then after they start the work, they inform you that they made a mistake and the actual price is higher than all the other bidders. At this point, it's difficult for you to fight with them or fire them and get another (sub) contractor to finish the job. Most often, the homebuyer simply pays the price. If the bid is higher than the others, the (sub) contractor made a mistake or is very busy and doesn't really want your job. He figures that if he gets it at that price, the profit margin will be so large that he can't turn down the job.

If you're using these bids to negotiate with your homebuilder, drop the high and low bids and average the bids that fall in the middle. If you're picking a (sub) contractor, pick one whose bid price fell in the low end of the middle; don't necessarily go with the low bidder.

If all the bidders are within 10% (plus or minus) of each other, that range is a good indication of what it costs to build your project. Most (sub) contractors keep close track of the "street" price. If they're going to compete on bids, they need to have competitive prices. Contractors often call other contractors to get bids on a fictitious job to see how their prices compare to their competitors—this ploy is called "secret shopping."

When a (sub) contractor bids a job, he has more cost control on some line items than others. He controls his billable labor rates for the number of hours and the per-hour charge. He controls off-the-shelf item prices because he usually gets them at a large margin and often buys them in bulk and warehouses them. He has lower profit margins and can negotiate less for special-order materials and subcontractor prices on their labor and materials.

When you look at the line items on the returned bids, think about what this (sub) contractor has control over and what he doesn't. This comparison gives you a better idea of how much you might be able to negotiate with him.

A 10-Minute Negotiation Can Save You $10,000

I know I've said it already: Negotiate. Bidding is another good place for negotiation. (Sub) contractors are the same as anyone else providing a product or service. Certain circumstances increase your ability to negotiate. For example, if a (sub) contractor doesn't have enough work scheduled for his crews, had a job drop out of queue, has trouble collecting on his accounts payable or lost money on a job, wants to expand, or wants to buy a new truck or piece of equipment, he'll be more flexible in his pricing because he needs your job more. Remember, you have nothing to lose, and a 10-minute conversation can save you 10% of your budget.

note I understand how difficult it is at first to negotiate. I never met anyone who felt comfortable the first few times he or she tried it. Negotiation gets easier the more you do it, however, and can even be fun. Try kidding around while negotiating. Ask for the "family price" or the "employee discount." Say "come on" a lot, and ask, "Where can we save some money here?" Don't take the first answer you get as the end. Wear them down. Keep asking. Don't be afraid; contractors are used to it. That's what they do all day with subs and suppliers. They actually get a kick out of you negotiating with them. Watch them: They'll smile when you start. The first time you're successful and save a thousand dollars, you'll see how much fun it can be.

The Importance of Including Your Specs and Selects

You might be getting tired of hearing about specs and selects, but they can be useful during the process of comparing bids from (sub) contractors. The more complex the project, the more difficult it is to compare apples to apples. If a (sub) contractor misses only one line item, it could create an error in the bid and lower the total bid cost by as much as 20%. By including the specifications for your project, you can help ensure that every (sub) contractor's bid includes all your criteria; however, it's no guarantee that all line items are accounted for in the bid. You still have to check.

Some less reputable (sub) contractors might leave an item off their bid to make their bid come in as the lowest one. If they win the bid, sometimes they bill you extra after the project is underway and you're committed. In most cases, however, overlooking a line item is simply an error. Whether the oversight is intentional or not, if that line item is necessary to your project, someone has to pay for it.

When you receive the bids, look over the line items. Check to see whether they include items or labor you didn't think of. Be sure that all bids contain the same line items. If there are missing or unnecessary items, have those (sub) contractors make the corrections and rebid on your project. Rebidding the project costs them time and money and requires very little time on your part. As I said previously, you'll probably have only one high bid and one low bid, so at most you'll need to make only two phone calls. Asking for corrected bids ensures that when you compare the bid totals, they're similar enough for a fair comparison.

Three Ways to Minimize the Impact of Bid Errors

If the project has already started with the (sub) contractor you chose, and he tells you an item was missing or some other error was made in the bid requiring additional expenses, renegotiating at that point is difficult. (Sub) contractors know that. You have already signed a contract preventing you from hiring someone else, even though the contract also holds your (sub) contractor to that fixed price. In either case, your (sub) contractor probably won't be able to complete your project for the agreed-on price. It's up to you to decide whether it's in your best interest to hold the (sub) contractor to his original bid price or compromise.

If the difference is minimal, you can insist that your (sub) contractor honor the price in the contract and "eat" the loss or make it up out of his profits. If it's more substantial, you probably don't want him to work on your project knowing that he'll have to do everything possible to cut corners and save his time and money. In this case, there are three ways, discussed in the following sections, to help prevent or at least minimize the impact to you and your budget.

Minimize Bid Errors with Specs and Selects

The first way to minimize the impact is to include your homebuilder's specs (or ones you create yourself) when you ask (sub) contractors to bid on your project. Having the specs handy assists them in addressing every line item and helps keep the bids similar for comparison. Including your specs isn't a guarantee that nothing gets overlooked or omitted, but it certainly helps.

Minimize Bid Errors with a "Not to Exceed" Clause

The second way to minimize the impact is to include a "not to exceed" clause in your contract. Often (sub) contractors include verbiage that allow them to charge for "unforeseen" problems, such as an excavator's contract specifying the possibility of additional charges if he unexpectedly runs into undocumented underground utilities, rock, or ground water. These circumstances can add significantly to the excavator's time and expense.

To counter these "unforeseen" charges, most bids include a "not to exceed" clause at the end of the contract that states, "The price quoted is an estimate and not to exceed more than 10% of the total estimated amount." Of course, this percentage can vary, but you're protected if something does go wrong or if there was an error in the bid. You never have to pay more than the "not to exceed" percentage specified in the contract. Try to get your (sub) contractor to eliminate the additional percentage from the quote and keep it a flat "not to exceed." If your (sub) contractor insists on a percent or an amount, keep it small because it's an open invitation to charge you that additional money.

Minimize Bid Errors with a Time and Materials (T&M) Clause

Another way to protect yourself against exorbitant mid-project charges and to be fair to your (sub) contractor, thus ensuring a better job, is specifying an agreed-on hourly rate for extras in the contract. These extras might be unexpected work that's needed as you proceed through the project; often it's additional work you request that falls outside the agreed-on bid amount. As your homebuilder does, your (sub) contractor should ask you to sign off on all change orders or work authorizations. These forms help both you and your (sub) contractor keep track of any additional expenses during the course of construction.

Be sure to ask for an estimate or even a "not to exceed" quote on the extra work for which you're paying time and materials (T&M). Hourly rates can add up, especially if the (sub) contractor is slow or runs into problems.

Most contracts also include a paragraph describing T&M for any work that's not covered by the contract. This paragraph specifies the hourly rate for different types of work that can be performed and includes materials. After you and your (sub) contractor have agreed on the rate, you can monitor the additional expenses, if any, to be billed.

As you did with your homebuilder, make sure (sub) contractors come with references and insurance and are bonded and licensed.

Does Your Homebuilder Mark Up Outside Bids?

As I mentioned, your homebuilder is a good source of recommendations for (sub) contractors you should hire because he usually has relationships with these people. Inevitably, a question about those relationships comes up, however. If my homebuilder suggests that I use his swimming pool contractor and I do, for example, does my homebuilder get a kickback from the pool company?

Using a referral from your homebuilder is almost always a good idea, as long as you get a good price. Your homebuilder sends business to subcontractors and vice versa. Because they have establishing a working relationship, these subcontractors listen to your homebuilder, do favors for him, schedule around him, and maybe even reduce prices or add incentives, all because they want your homebuilder's referral business. The cost of acquiring a new customer for any business is significant.

THE COST OF CUSTOMER ACQUISITION

The cost of acquiring a new customer is a major expense for all product and service sales companies. It's often referred to as *customer acquisition cost* or *customer acquisition and retention cost* and varies a great deal from company to company. For example, the customer acquisition cost for a credit card company is around $150 in marketing and advertising expenses. The customer acquisition cost is why credit card companies in competition for your business eliminate their annual fees, lower their monthly interest rates, and drop service fees and late charges if you ask; they don't want to incur the $150 cost of replacing you as a customer. That's also why they are so persistent about calling you if you close your account.

Here are some other examples of customer acquisition costs: Nextel's is $430, XM Satellite Radio's is $123, DirecTV's is around $550, and TD Waterhouse averages $175. Mortgage companies spend between $300 and $700 for each funded mortgage, and a homebuilder can spend $2,300 per new homebuyer.

The answer to the question of whether your homebuilder is getting a kickback from your referral is probably. When your homebuilder refers you to a swimming pool builder and you agree to have him construct your new pool, you become a new customer without any expense to that pool builder. This additional margin can be paid back to your homebuilder as a referral fee or finder's fee. The big question is whether you're paying that finder's fee or it's coming out of the pool builder's advertising budget or profits. The best way to learn that is to do your "home" work.

How Much Markup Is Fair?

No amount of markup is fair. You shouldn't have to pay anything to cover a referral or finder's fee. That should be between your homebuilder and the pool builder (or other subcontractor). You should get a great pool at a great price. To find out whether this relationship could wind up costing you something, refer to the section "When You Compare, You Know the Facts" earlier in this chapter.

After you have determined the type, size, and design for your swimming pool, ask your potential pool builder to give you an itemized cost breakdown. Contact several other pool building companies, fax them a design and the specs, and ask for a quote. *Don't send them the costs from the original bid!* If you do, they will simply come back with a dollar amount matching those costs or one that's only slightly lower to beat the bid. You want to know the fair "street" price is for building your pool.

When you receive two or more bids, compare them. If the bid from the pool company your homebuilder referred you to is lower, go with that company. If not, call that pool builder and ask why his bid isn't lower. He might have made an error in the numbers or made an error by assuming you would never know. Either way, by comparing the bids, you can get the best swimming pool at the best price, and if you choose your builder's referral, that pool builder will be sure to stay on schedule and do a good job for you.

These kickbacks or referral fees apply to subcontractor referrals by your homebuilder but also include work that your homebuilder is subcontracting. For upgrades or add-ons that your homebuilder isn't doing but is getting subcontractor prices for you, before you say yes to the subcontractor your homebuilder recommends, compare his costs by following the previous recommendations to fax a few bid requests to check the price. Additional examples of these items can include fireplace surrounds, spa and whirlpool tubs, surround sound, security systems, water softeners, smart home electronics, outdoor misting systems, chiminias (outdoor fireplaces and fire pits), boat docks, garage floor epoxy finishes, and so on.

Summary

Getting bids from (sub) contractors isn't as scary as it might seem. When you compare bids from (sub) contractors, you need to know the facts and make sure the facts being compared are the same for all bids. To help you do this, you can include your plans and your specs and selects in materials you send out to (sub) contractors.

Remember: Costs aren't cast in concrete, and (sub) contractors' bids are negotiable like everything else. This chapter also explained three ways you can lessen the impact of unexpected costs in your project after you have accepted a bid.

Working with Change Orders

14

Change orders can change the way you think about you new home. All home-builders dislike change orders, some won't even consider them, and others charge you just to accept them.

As you go through the process of building your new home, you'll see the home come alive as part of the process of going from a two-dimensional drawing to a three-dimensional home. Not all your ideas will look the same when they're actually built. At times, you might want to change something, such as a window size or location, a closet enlargement, or a doorway to an arched opening.

You need to understand what your homebuilder will accept as a change, what he won't accept, and how much it will cost you.

What Are Change Orders?

Change orders are a reality of all construction projects and need to be addressed head on. With the complexity of building your new home, it's inevitable that something will be missed, could be done better, or could simply be changed. A *change order* is a simple document, generally one sheet, that amends the agreement between you and your

In this chapter:

* Understand what a change order is and how it affects you

* Discover how you can eliminate potential mis-understandings

* Learn who accepts a change order and when

* See why it's important to document and fax all conversations about change orders

* To find out how to download a free change order sheet, see page 4

homebuilder, describes the change, demonstrates that both you and your homebuilder agree on what the change is, specifies how long this change may or may not affect the construction schedule, details associated expenses, obligates one or both parties for the additional cost, and is signed by both parties.

Change orders can often be the beginning of the end of an otherwise good relationship between you and the homebuilder. Many disagreements stem from which party is responsible for the expense of carrying out the change and whether the cost is reasonable. The homebuyer often thinks that the homebuilder is making huge profits on change orders, but the homebuilder seldom breaks even. Many times he has to stop construction, reschedule subcontractors, redesign, and reorder materials for even the simplest change. The homebuilder is also required to follow through with the administrative side of change orders: preparing the work for bid, collecting the bids, calculating the costs involved, completing the paperwork, securing your approval and signature, and then supervising the new work to be sure it's completed correctly and on time.

The key to maintaining a good working relationship with your homebuilder and avoiding possible sticker shock is to communicate constantly with your homebuilder. Change orders, by definition, mean more cost to you and more confusion to your homebuilder. Discuss any change you have with your homebuilder until you're comfortable with the cost and any potential delays needed to complete the change.

Change orders can occur for many reasons. Homebuyers often have difficulty looking at a two-dimensional set of blueprints and visualizing what the home will look like or how it will function, so they want to modify a room layout, a closet size, or a window placement, for example. Also, the homebuilder might miss something in the specs and selects that aren't communicated to a framer, electrician, plumber, or other subcontractor.

Unforeseen circumstances can also require change orders. For example, a building code change might require something to be constructed differently. Other unexpected reasons for change orders include soil conditions, such as ground water and underground rock; labor or material shortages; new product releases; and out-of-stock and discontinued items. Changes that come as a surprise usually result in additional expenses for the homebuyer.

Work not done in sequence costs more than work that's done routinely. Change order work, on average, costs 10% to 15% more than the same work done on a normal construction schedule. Work estimated on a change order is analyzed more carefully than work carried out under the original agreement. Change orders are often calculated with exacting amounts under each heading of labor, material, delivery, subcontracts, taxes, coordination, supervision, permits, testing, insurance, bonds, overhead, and profit. Homebuilders know that change orders are scrutinized under a microscope.

As the homebuyer, you have the right to change your mind. Just be prepared: Each change has an associated cost, can cause a delay, and presents a communication challenge.

The best way to reduce the number of change orders or eliminate them is to think through each aspect of your project. When working with the New Home Ideas Workbook, visualize how your selects go together, have your homebuilder answers any questions you might have about the house plans, study your brochures, look at model homes, review your photographs, and walk the job site a few times per week. All these measures help you visualize what your new home should look like.

> **note** *Errors to Avoid* Not all change orders result in additional expenses for homebuyers. Some changes can actually save you money. Bear this in mind when discussing a change order with your homebuilder. If a change results in a savings on materials or labor, that savings should be passed on to you.

When Can You Do Change Orders?

Most change orders can be accepted at any time during construction. Of course, the sooner you submit a change order, the better. You don't want to ask to have a wall moved or have additional electrical work done after the drywall has been installed. Your homebuilder can do almost anything at any point in the building process, but the longer you wait, the more construction will have taken place and the more collateral damage there will be during the change, resulting in a higher expense to you.

The best way to schedule a change order is not to have one at all. Walk your job site and meet with your homebuilder regularly. Finding time for these activities might be difficult because of your and your homebuilder's schedules, but try. The sooner you catch a change that needs to be made, the less expensive it is to carry out.

When you first sign your agreement with your homebuilder, ask him to go through your construction schedule and point out where the milestones are. For example, have him explain when the walls will be enclosed and which changes aren't feasible after that point. Ask him to show you when the drywall texturing will be completed so that you know when to change any decisions on paint colors for walls, which is the next step of construction.

Knowing where the cut-off points are gives you the maximum amount of time to change your mind while minimizing the cost of that change.

Who Accepts Change Orders?

Be prepared: Some homebuilders don't accept change orders. Change orders add another level of confusion for your homebuilder and another possibility for mistakes. They often require rescheduling some subcontractors and delaying others. I have never heard of a homebuilder actually making money on a change order; most homebuilders just hope to at least break even on them. Before you sign an agreement with your homebuilder, have a conversation about the rules for change orders. Some homebuilders accept a change order up to a certain date and not after. Some homebuilders accept change orders only for certain items, and some charge you $250 in addition to the cost of the work just to accept the change order. Be sure you understand your homebuilder's rules before you sign an agreement.

Custom homebuilders are accustomed to change orders because they build homes to suit the homebuyers. Sometimes that means making changes while construction is underway. Custom homebuilders are accommodating and will change almost anything at any time—for a fee.

Semi-custom homebuilders accept change orders but on a more limited scale. Most of a semi-custom home's design is fixed, so you can change the color of a wall but not move that wall, for example. You can submit change orders for minor items, such as your selects for paint or tile color, interior door styles, garage door type, and kitchen cabinets. You just can't make changes to the structure, such as room sizes, layout, ceiling heights, architectural style, or number of bathrooms. Semi-custom homebuilders might be willing to make these changes, but they can be expensive.

Production homebuilders rarely accept change orders. When a home is designed and manufactured off site, changes are nearly impossible. A typical production homebuilder isn't able to consider major changes. The framer assembles the framing, but he doesn't actually build the frame from scratch, for example. The electrician and other subcontractors are on a budget so tight, they can't add an electrical receptacle or add the time to install it.

Be sure to ask your homebuilder the following questions:

- What can I change during the course of construction?
- What can't I change?
- At which points during construction does it become cost prohibitive to make changes? And what types of changes are cost prohibitive?
- Do you charge me just to accept a change order?
- How long does it take from the time we agree on a change to when I get the estimate?

To do list

- ☐ Review your house plans early.
- ☐ Identify anything you want changed.
- ☐ Walk your job site.
- ☐ Communicate any changes early and clearly with your homebuilder.
- ☐ Thoroughly document any change you want made.

Always Communicate Your Change Orders

As always, good communication is essential. Be sure to get your homebuilder's attention, discuss changes with him, have him repeat changes to you, ask him to give you a rough nonbinding estimate of the time and costs involved as soon as possible, and have him fax or mail you a copy of the change order to eliminate any potential misunderstandings.

Avoid Unwritten Change Orders

A big pitfall of change orders is the unwritten change order, which occurs when the homebuyer asks for a change while walking the job site with the homebuilder or during a phone call to the homebuilder's office. The change usually takes place almost immediately if the subcontractor performing that task is on site and can react quickly. This saves the homebuilder and subcontractor additional scheduling and travel time, which saves you money. The homebuyer anticipates that the paperwork and associated expense for that change will be forwarded to the homebuilder's attention quickly, but often this isn't the case.

In many instances, you might not be made aware of potential scheduling delays and additional costs until after the change order work has already been done. When this happens, it's common to hear homebuyers say, "I never would have authorized that change if I'd known it was going to cost me that much time and money." By then, however, it's too late—the work is done. Your homebuilder insists that you authorized him to make that change. You insist you wouldn't have if you had known how much it would cost, and around you go. Who's right and who's wrong?

You both are, but that won't help the situation. The best way to resolve this conflict is not to allow it to happen in the first place. As the homebuyer who ultimately pays for the change, take the responsibility to find out as quickly as possible what the associated expenses will be, preferably before the work is done. If your homebuilder can't respond that quickly, ask him to estimate the expense, and then have his office fax the estimate to you or at least have him explain the costs to you in front of another person.

If the work has already been done, keeping calm and communicating with your homebuilder are the most important things you can do. Discuss the charges in detail, and ask if there's any way he can tighten costs on a material or labor line items (negotiate) until you reach a mutually acceptable outcome. The alternatives are paying full price or creating a legal battle. Remember: Anything other than a compromise costs you far more than a compromise would.

HOW CHANGE ORDERS CAN GO WRONG

Here's an actual example of how change orders can go awry. I had just supervised the framing of a Mission/Santa Fe–style home and asked the homebuyers to walk the job site with the electrical contractor and me to discuss any changes or add-ons they might want to make while the walls were completely open and easy to work on.

Typically, I suggest receptacles (outlets) near the roof for easy installation of Christmas lights without extension cords, rear floodlights for illuminating the backyard for parties and for security purposes, motion sensors, and low-voltage lighting to wash an interior wall and to light pot shelves and above the kitchen cabinets. My favorite suggestion is to install a ceiling fan in the master bathroom as a nice touch for getting dressed after showering (really cools you off and helps when applying makeup—for my wife, not me).

During this walkthrough, I was called away to answer a question from the HVAC (heating, ventilation, and air-conditioning) subcontractor. When I returned, the homebuyer and electrician were finishing up and assured me that everything had been discussed and was under control.

Six months later, when it was time to turn the home over to the homebuyers, they got the bill for the electrical change order and freaked out. I didn't blame them. The additional expense was thousands of dollars. The electrician was happy to keep adding items to his change order list, so he encouraged the homebuyers without explaining the associated expenses. Each additional receptacle cost $150, and additional fan boxes (excluding the fan and light fixture) were another $150 each. The costs added up fast. The electrician did the work and billed the homebuilder, and he had to bill the homebuyers.

How can you avoid this problem? Ask how much each change will cost, and ask for a change order outlining the expense in detail before the work begins.

Fax, Fax, Fax Your Conversations

Here's another tip I have to stress again: Fax, fax, fax.

Every time you and your homebuilder discuss a change in design, costs, layout, color, texture, additional items, or any other changes, document the conversation. Carry a pad and pencil when you walk the job site. Bring them with you when you go to your homebuilder's office or meet him for coffee.

When you return home or to your office, open your word processor, type up a brief summary of what you and your homebuilder discussed and agreed on, add the date, and then fax the document to your homebuilder. Make sure you print a copy to keep in your folder. Most computers have a built-in fax modem and a word-processing program, and the phone call for the fax is most likely local. It's all free and takes only a few moments. If you don't have a built-in fax, you can always use your local copy shop or mailbox store.

By faxing a summary of your conversation with your homebuilder, you can accomplish a great deal. You're reiterating your understanding of what you agreed to. If your fax explanation is different from what your homebuilder thought he said, now's the time to find that out and get it rectified. If you both agree, you have helped him document what you discussed so that there are no misunderstandings later. A faxed summary also gives your homebuilder a written document outlining your requests and his approval, so he and his office staff can follow up on it more easily. This document also ensures that he and his staff have a reminder, so they won't overlook it. It also produces a paper trail so that if there's any misunderstanding about whether your homebuilder agreed to the change or what the associated costs would be, the agreement is in writing and dated. All this peace of mind is free.

Summary

In this chapter, you have learned what a change order is and how to avoid misunderstandings when working with change orders. You've also learned the right and wrong times to carry out change orders and who does and doesn't accept change orders.

This chapter has also explained the importance of documenting all conversations about changes with your homebuilder. Faxing a dated summary of these conversations to your homebuilder helps ensure that your changes are carried out with your homebuilder's cooperation and done correctly, on time, and for the amount you agreed to.

See "Additional Resources" on page 4 for details on how to download a free change order sheet.

The Importance of Your Financial Draws

The *construction draw process* is important to your homebuilder; it enables him to get paid for materials and work he and his subcontractors have performed in small, scheduled, and defined payments. The *construction draw schedule* specifies when he gets paid for building your new home in incremental amounts for the work he has completed. It's a way to control the amount of money given to your homebuilder at one time, which helps him pay his subs and suppliers, controls the quality of work being performed, and limits potential liability to both you and your lender.

Following a construction draw schedule reduces the possibility that your homebuilder could decide to take off with your funds and not finish your home. The draw schedule regulates the payment process to protect you.

How the Draw Process Works

When you get approved for a new home construction loan, your lender sets aside the total amount of money you have available. During the course of construction, your homebuilder submits what's called a *construction draw schedule* that outlines the work he will perform and the costs for that work.

In this chapter:

* Learn what a construction draw is and why it's important
* See how the construction draw process works to protect you
* Understand how your funds are released
* Learn how a line-item draw schedule can prevent project delays if a draw item is missed

Draws are generally divided into five separate payments that are accessible when certain percentages of the construction schedule are completed. At the completion of each portion, your homebuilder notifies you and your lender. Your lender hires an inspector to visit your new home site and verifies that all the work described in the construction draw schedule up to that point has been performed. After your lender receives verification from the inspector, that portion of the funds is released to your homebuilder. He can then pay his subs, suppliers, and himself.

When you apply for and are approved for a new home construction loan, this loan is often called a construction-to-permanent loan. That means you're issued portions of your total loan amount as your new home is constructed. When your new home is completed, the balance is distributed, and the loan becomes a standard home loan secured by the equity in your new home and the land it's built on. The term or length of your construction loan begins on the date you sign your loan documents.

At the time you close on your loan, you're usually asked to sign a construction disbursement account information form that identifies the bank account you have opened for receiving these wired funds. Then you receive funding (a money transfer) into that account, usually within 24 hours, that covers all your off-site ("soft") costs, excluding your builder's overhead. No other cash disbursement is made until the home is approximately 10% to 15% complete and your lender receives a copy of your building permit.

During the course of construction and throughout the draw process, your homebuilder invoices your lender directly unless you contract with a subcontractor or purchase materials yourself. If you have prepaid items that are reflected in your budget, they might be considered an equity contribution and not reimbursable in your construction loan. For example, say you find a floor tile medallion (an intricate mosaic design typically used in entryways), and buy it yourself to have the tile company install it. The lender might consider this a prepurchase or equity investment in your new home and not want to reimburse you for it in your construction loan. Be sure to speak with your lender about reimbursement before you purchase or subcontract anything.

On your homebuilder's invoice, he generally charges items to one of three categories: on-site costs, off-site costs, and deposits.

On-site costs, also known as "direct costs" or "hard costs," are associated with the actual labor and materials used for the construction of your new home. On-site costs are actual costs accrued during the construction of your new home project instead of the estimated line items allocated in the budget (which are discussed later in "Set Your Draws on Line Items").

Off-site costs are indirect expenses (soft costs) not directly related to labor or materials for construction and, as a result, can't go through inspections. Some examples of off-site costs include building permits, water meter fees, soil reports, termite treatments, and architectural fees.

Reimbursements to your homebuilder for his vendors for items such as kitchen cabinets, light fixtures, floor tile, and any specialty improvements that require custom craftsmanship usually require *deposits*. Some lenders release only up to 50% of the total amount budgeted for a specific line item for deposits and will require receipt of vendor invoices.

Inspections and Release of Funds

Disbursements on your construction loan are designed to reimburse your homebuilder as construction of your new home progresses. Lenders disburse construction proceeds based on the amount of work that has been completed on the project and specified on your homebuilder's construction draw schedule. For example, if your total construction budget has been approved at $200,000 and your project is at the 10% draw stage, the lender disburses up to $20,000 on your project to your homebuilder.

When your new home has been constructed to the stage determined in your construction draw schedule, your homebuilder can request his draw amount. He completes a written draw request and faxes it to your lender. When the lender receives your homebuilder's draw request, he immediately orders an inspection to verify the status of construction on your home. These inspections are usually done within three to five business days and have no associated fee.

The percentage completed is based on the inspector's verification. The lender hires a qualified construction home inspector (or has one on staff) who can determine the quality of work and accurately certify that all line items on your homebuilder's construction schedule have been completed successfully. Each homebuilder disbursement or draw is in addition to any advances or deposits you might be entitled to receive. All disbursements for on-site direct cost expenses need to be verified by an inspection before your lender transfers those funds.

When your lender receives notice from the inspector that the percentage of completion and quality of work have been verified, the lender contacts your title company to verify that that your property is free of any mechanic's liens (see the Note in this section for more on mechanic's liens). If it is, your lender issues funds to you so that you can write your homebuilder a check for that portion of the project.

It's important to realize that you're responsible for your funds at all times. You control payments to your homebuilder, who in turn pays his subs and suppliers. Ultimately, you're the one who needs to be satisfied before your homebuilder gets paid. The timing of payments varies from lender to lender, but usually you can get disbursements from your lender within 48 hours or less of your lender receiving verification from the inspector and the title company.

Your final draw comes when your new home is between 95% and 100% complete. Approximately 10% of the overall amount of your funds is generally retained in your account until the closing of your new home when you legally take ownership. At this point, you can hold the funds to be sure your new home is complete, built to your satisfaction, and completed without any major errors. After you have taken possession of your new home and are satisfied with its construction, you can release the remaining funds to pay your homebuilder in full.

For your homebuilder to receive his final payment, he must provide your lender with a copy of the Certificate of Occupancy (C of O) if applicable, a copy of the septic certificate, and the final draw request. You're required to provide a copy of your current proof of homeowner's insurance in the amount of the newly valued structure.

> **note** A *mechanic's lien* is a legal debt attached to or placed on your real estate (land) that secures the payment of debts due to people who have performed labor or services or furnished materials or supplies for the construction of your new home. This lien can be filed by anyone who has worked on your new home or provided materials and hasn't been paid, including your homebuilder (if he doesn't get paid or if he doesn't pay his suppliers or subcontractors).
>
> To remove a mechanic's lien from your property, you must pay the full amount of the lien or have a legal judgment releasing you of that liability.

At this point, your lender "rolls" your loan over to a conventional mortgage, and you begin making monthly payments on the total loan amount for the period you agreed to. Then it's just a standard conventional loan.

Miss a Schedule, Miss a Draw, Slow the Progress

The five-draw schedule is an industry standard and works well in most cases. It protects you from poor workmanship and having your money taken without the work being performed. The inherent problem with this system is in the construction draw schedule itself. For your homebuilder to request one of his draws, all the work outlined on the construction draw schedule must be completed and verified by your lender's inspector. Sounds like a good thing, but the problem happens when one or more of the scheduled line items haven't been completed.

Often, during the course of construction, many items can't be completed at the time they should be for different reasons. A common example is when the house is at its 75% to 80% completion mark, and your homebuilder is ready to ask for his fourth draw. The inspector visits your new home to verify that all items called for in that draw segment have been completed and sees that the kitchen cabinets haven't been installed yet. Because kitchen cabinets are hand-crafted and can take extra time, this delay is quite common, especially in this building boom market.

The problem occurs when this draw is refused until the cabinetry is finished. Everything else has been finished and construction could continue, but no more funds are released until the cabinets are installed. In some cases, it could take a month or more for the cabinetmaker to catch up. Without the draw, the homebuilder can't pay his subs or suppliers for the work already performed to date, and no work can continue or be started without funding. Your project could come to a complete stop. Not to worry, however—there's a solution.

Set Your Draws on Line Items

More homebuilders are requesting that your lender provide what's called a *line-item draw*. It's still based on a standard construction draw schedule, but each item has an associated expense listed with it.

In the situation with kitchen cabinets mentioned previously, if the cabinetmaker is behind schedule, your homebuilder could still ask for a partial draw that includes all line items except the cabinets. This way, your homebuilder can pay his subs and suppliers and keep moving on your project with other tasks. He could continue with installing floor tile, completing the exterior final stucco coat, installing your roof, and maybe finish painting or completing the rough grading of the job site. With a line-item draw, a missing item doesn't affect your project or your homebuilder's cash flow.

To use this option, you have to ask your lender to set up your construction loan on a line-item draw basis. Many lenders don't tell you about this option and many won't do it for you. With a line-item draw, your lender has to keep track of many more items than just the five typical draws. A line-item draw is more work for them. However, if you can get your lender to agree to this type of draw schedule, it helps keep your project moving.

Other Draw Items You Should Know About

Construction loans are calculated and paid a little differently than a conventional mortgage. Because funds are disbursed a portion at a time, you have to pay only the interest on the monies you have used to date, not the entire amount of the loan. The interest accrues only on the distributed funds. You are, however, required to make payments on that interest on a monthly basis. If you miss these payments, all future disbursements are stopped, which means the construction also stops until this problem is solved.

A problem that often comes up is a new home construction project running into delays and the home isn't completed before the construction loan's termination date. If this happens, technically you're in default on your construction loan agreement. Because this problem happens so often, your lender is usually willing to work with you to grant an extension. Keep track of this termination date because if you do pass it, all loan draws are put on hold until the extension is granted. It's a good idea to contact your loan officer at least 30 days before the completion date if the construction isn't at least 95% complete so that he can begin the extension process.

Also, be aware that the extension might result in an additional fee that can represent 0.5% of the total loan amount for each month past the original completion date. If the delay is caused by your homebuilder, you might want to tell him that you expect him to pay this fee. If the delays were caused because you didn't make your selects on time or made changes that resulted in a delay, you should bear the additional cost. If the fee is 0.5% of $200,000, for example, the extra cost could total $1,000 per month.

Summary

This chapter has explained what a construction draw schedule is and why it's so important to you, your homebuilder, and his subs and suppliers. You've also learned how the construction draw process works to protect you and your new home.

You have seen how funds are released and learned that you have control over all your funds. In addition, you've learned about line-item draw schedules and how they can prevent project delays if a draw item is missed.

16

Building a Contingency into Your Loan

When you drive down the freeway and look at new homes in recently completed neighborhoods, have you ever seen bed sheets nailed up in bedroom windows? As often as you see this, you would think it's a new trend in interior design to coordinate your bed coverings with your window treatments. It's not. It's that the first night after moving in, the homebuyers started to get undressed and looked out the window at neighbors looking back. They ran to the garage, grabbed the yard-sale bed sheets, a hammer, and nails, and voilà—drapes.

To avoid having to wait until the next white sale to get window treatments for your new home, you need to plan ahead. That's where a "contingency" comes in.

In this chapter:

* Learn the three categories of unanticipated last-minute expenses
* See how you can build in insurance against these expenses
* If you don't use, you don't pay for it
* Understand how you can actually save money by using your contingency

Planning Ahead for Unseen Expenses

A *contingency* is planning for a "what if" or, more to the point, a "for when." A contingency is about setting some money aside from your loan, whether it's used at the end of your new home construction or not used at all.

During the course of building your new home, you need to make nearly 5,000 decisions. The New

Home Ideas Workbook can help you make these decisions and, I hope, not miss any. If you do, a contingency comes in handy. It's there to pay for any decision you didn't account for in your budget, and it's there for those "must have" upgrades.

Be Prepared for Upgrades, Unforeseen Events, and Unanticipated Necessities

There will be expenses that you just couldn't have anticipated. As you see your new home come together, piece by piece, you'll find three primary places where you might want to use your contingency.

The first place you might need to spend money not originally budgeted for is on upgrades. Maybe you would like a bigger window over the kitchen sink or a bigger pantry. Maybe while looking for lighting fixtures, you find the chandelier of your dreams, or you want to upgrade the refrigerator to the top-of-the-line model you saw in the showroom. All these improvements have an associated cost that wasn't included in your initial budget.

The second place where you might need a contingency is for events you couldn't possibly have planned for. A common example is hitting rock while digging for your foundation, utilities trench, or septic tank. Another example is a last-minute increase in prices on an item you ordered, such as kitchen tile or plumbing fixtures. You might also encounter a code change requiring you to build something that wasn't in your new home's original bid price. Any of these unforeseen events that occur during construction of your new home cost extra to resolve. If your building budget is being spent down to your last dollar, you won't

note Code changes in your area can add to the cost of your home in unexpected ways. The City of Phoenix and surrounding areas passed ordinances requiring that all new swimming pools have a 5-foot-high childproof fence built around them and that all new fireplaces be gas operated and have a sealed fire chamber (sealed glass across the front to prevent air from the living space from combusting and going up the chimney).

have the money available to fix these problems, and if you're like most new homebuyers, your construction loan is the maximum amount of money you can afford to borrow. That's why planning a contingency amount into your loan allows you to make upgrade decisions without worrying about how you will pay for them.

The third place where contingencies come in handy is at the end of construction, when homebuyers have moved in and discover they need additional furnishings or features. At this point, people often realize they have no window coverings or need window tinting. Or maybe you think, "Wow, the front yard landscaping looks great, but the back yard is dirt from fence to fence! It just rained, and I have two dogs, three kids, and mud everywhere." You might also discover you need closet organizers, awnings, fountains, low-voltage exterior and security lighting, a boat dock, a barbecue grill, irrigation, a tool shed or workshop, garage shelving, walkways, patio furniture, or even a spa or swimming pool. Typically, these features are either things you didn't think of when planning your new home or things you thought you could add later but didn't realize how important they would be.

Build It into the Loan So That It Can Be Built into the House

There are two ways to protect yourself against running out of cash: Use some discipline when spending, and set some money aside just in case. I understand that both are easier said than done when building your new dream home, but they can be done. I won't address the first issue, as I'm sure spending discipline has a 12-step program or its own wing at the Betty Ford Clinic, but setting aside some money is an issue I can help you with. If you're looking for help with spending wisely, take a look at http://www.smartmoneytips.com, "Helpful Resources for Smart Money Management."

When you work with your lender and set up a budget for building your new home, ask your lender to set aside a contingency. Make it a line item just as though it were something in the budget that needed to be paid for. Don't spend your entire budget on the house—not yet. After the contingency money has been allocated, don't touch it until you absolutely have to or only at the very end of your building project.

Based on my experience in homebuilding, you should budget at least $15,000 and preferably $20,000 (or 5% to 10%) of your house price for your contingency line item.

If You Don't Use All the Money, You Can Give It Back

The next logical question I'm asked is, "Okay, if I need the extra money, I have it, but what if I don't need it or I have some left over? I don't want to pay for money I didn't need for the next 30 years in my mortgage."

Not to worry. Remember in Chapter 15, "The Importance of Your Financial Draws," that I explained you pay only for the money you take from your lender each month. The same is true for a contingency fund. This money is in your budget only as a line item. You don't actually get the money until you need it, if at all.

If you finish building your new home and never need to touch that money, it isn't disbursed to you. Because it was never loaned to you, it's simply not included when your final loan amount is calculated. This way, you have the security of having an extra $20,000 available at any time during construction, but it doesn't cost you a thing unless you use it. Pretty cheap insurance!

Another big advantage of having a contingency built into your loan amount is that if you do need to use some of the money for, say, window treatments, the cost is added to your final home mortgage. This means the cost of your window coverings is amortized over a 30-year period. In other words, you can have custom window treatment immediately and for much less money than if you put the cost on your credit card (assuming you have a card with any remaining limit left).

Say you're spending $5,000 on custom window treatments for your new home. These two scenarios show how a contingency can work for you:

Scenario 1: You have window treatments designed and created, and the charge is added to your credit card. Because credit cards are amortized on a one-year (12 month/12 payment) basis, your monthly payment at 18% costs $458.40 per month for those new window treatments.

Scenario 2: You decide to use part of your contingency for designing and creating new window treatments. At the time of closing on your permanent loan, your lender includes the $5,000 contingency expense in your final mortgage amount. Assuming a 30-year mortgage at 5%, your window treatments cost only $26.84 per month.

With the current IRS rules of deductions, very little can qualify as a deduction. Interest on your home mortgage is still deductible, however. Depending on your income tax bracket and specific situation, $20.83 of the monthly $26.84 would come back to you as tax-deductible interest.

Set aside a contingency fund. I recommend $20,000, but even $10,000 is going to help a lot.

Summary

In this chapter, you have learned about the three categories of unanticipated last-minute expenses that might catch you offguard if you don't prepare for them ahead of time. You can build in insurance against these expenses by having your lender set up a contingency line item in your loan amount.

Remember from what you learned about draws that if you don't use the money you set aside, you don't have to take it, and you won't have to pay for it. You also saw by comparing two scenarios of buying custom window treatments that you can actually save money by using your contingency.

Part IV

Planning and Prevention Will Build a Better Home

17

Understanding Building Permits and Approvals

Before you begin building your new home, you must apply for and receive your approved building permit. Your local governing municipality's building department grants your building permit after going through the "submittal" process and getting approval on the building plans for your new home. Even though filing for your building permit is your home-builder's responsibility, I'll walk you through the process so that you can better understand what's involved.

What You Need to Submit to Acquire a Building Permit

The building, planning, and safety department for your local town, city, or unincorporated county can provide the necessary plan review services for your new home building permit. The plan examiners and development engineering teams conduct comprehensive and detailed examinations of your plan submittals for development (building) permits. Projects are reviewed for compliance and conformance to local municipal ordinances, regulations, policies, and adopted safety codes.

The following list shows the typical type and quantity of documents the building department requires for a building permit submittal package. Be sure to contact your building department for its specific requirements:

- Provide four rolled complete sets of building plans (usually 24×36-inch format), which include calculations, specifications, equipment cut sheets, foundation plan, floor plan, and roof framing plans. You might also need to include a front-to-rear cross section of your house.

- Provide a fully dimensioned site plan, drawn to scale, including all fences, property lines, right-of-way centerline measurements, and easements.

- Provide the project's street address on all plans. Building needs to be identified by using city-assigned address numbers.

- Include a cover sheet with an index (supplied by the building department). Ensure that all sheets listed in the index are included and complete.

- Specify livable area and other roof areas separately in square feet, and separate different stories.

- Supply the minimum required building setbacks (the distance from the property lines to the nearest structure), with front, rear, and side views.

- A copy of the soil report must be included with the plan submittal.

- Include a completed permit application, a contractor's license verification, a certificate of insurance, and all applicable fees.

> **note** If you want to explore dozens of sample submittal forms, codes, and regulations, you can visit http://www.BetterHomesSeminars.com for free downloads of the City of Mesa, Arizona Building and Safety Department forms, or you can see them at http://www.ci.mesa.az.us/building_safety.

The fee for the plan review of your building permit varies, of course, from municipality to municipality, but fees are usually similar. Costs for plan reviews usually include the initial plan review and two resubmittals to accommodate any changes the building department might require. These fees are usually based on the total budgeted cost of the home you're building. Some municipalities accept your cost budget, or they might determine the cost value themselves based on their own cost-per-square-foot schedule.

Here are two examples of building permit fees for a 3,320 square foot home (at $128 per square foot) valued at $425,000. The first table is based on a home value the homebuilder provided, and the second table shows the value of the home based on the municipality's cost-per-square-foot calculations.

Valuation Fee Schedule

House Valuations	Permit Cost
Less than $1,000	$98.15 minimum
$1,000.00 to $50,000	$98.15 plus $13.42 for each additional $1,000
$50,000.01 to $100,000	$757.58 plus $11.19 for each additional $1,000
$100,000.01 to $150,000	$1,317.08 plus $10.07 for each additional $1,000
$150,000.01 to $200,000	$1,820.58 plus $ 9.08 for each additional $1,000
$200,000.01 to $300,000	$2,274.58 plus $ 8.10 for each additional $1,000
$300,000.01 to $400,000	$3,084.58 plus $ 6.72 for each additional $1,000
$400,000 or more	$3,757.36 plus $ 4.55 for each additional $1,000

This information is taken directly from the City of Mesa, Arizona Building Permit Fee Schedule.

The valuation example for this home results in a permit fee of $3,757.36 + ($4.55 × 25) or $3,871.11.

If the municipality calculated its own fee, it could look like the following table.

Permit Fee Based on Square Footage

Type of Space	Cost per Square Foot	Square Footage	Total
Living space	$58.95	3,320	$195,714
Entryway or covered patios	$13.77	550	$7,573
Garage	$20.25	600	$12,150
Total valuation			$215,437

Then you would calculate $2.95 per $100 valuation over $100,000 plus a $510 flat fee, as shown here:

$215,437 – $100,000 = $115,437

$115,437 ÷ $100 = $1,154.37

$1,154.37 × $2.95 = $3,405.39

$3,405.39 + $510 = $3,915.39 overall permit fee

This information is taken directly from the Town of Gilbert, Arizona, building permit fee schedule (the fastest growing town in America for two years running, as reported on CNN).

But that's not all. This is only the fee for the permit. There are also what municipalities call *impact fees*, which are one-time fees you pay for the impact or additional expense you create for the municipality's services. These fees can include what's listed in the following table.

Mesa, Arizona, Building Permit Impact Fees

Service	Fee
Cultural facility	$1,011
Wastewater	$1,289
Drinking water	$4,200
Parks and recreation	$962
Library	$424
General government facility	$446
Storm water drainage	$158
Fire	$145
Police	$226

In some cities, these fees can accumulate to more than $11,000 in additional expenses, which can bring the cost of your building permit to between $15,000 and $16,000. You need to work with your homebuilder to determine how much the fees will be in your specific municipality.

Who Should Submit Your Plans?

The good news about all these permits and fees is that it's your homebuilder's responsibility to complete all the forms, meet all the requirements, pay all the fees, and submit your building permit package.

In the beginning of the design phase of your new home, you work closely with your homebuilder or architect to develop the final designs that will be reflected in your house plans. After blueprints, specifications, and calculations are completed for your new home; your homebuilder takes the plans and cut sheets along with a check to your local building department.

Submitting your house plans so that you can be issued a building permit is your homebuilder's responsibility. I recommend that you don't get involved. This task is part of what your homebuilder's price for building your new home.

The Homebuilder Knows the System

There are many reasons that your homebuilder is the best person to submit your house plan for a building permit:

- He has the experience to answer any questions the building department has.
- He can fill out any forms or missing data on the spot.
- He can negotiate fees and requirements.
- He knows the best day and time to submit your plans.
- He knows deadlines, blackout dates, and holidays.
- He knows the people he's working with and they know him.

The last item in this list is an important one. Many times, I've seen a building department make an exception, extend a deadline, reduce a fee, expedite a review, overlook an error, and allow the homebuilder the opportunity to make the correction on the spot for a homebuilder who has a good reputation and has developed personal relationships with his municipal counterparts over the years. His reputation and relationship have a great deal of value to you.

How Long Can Permits Take?

Getting a building permit can be a lengthy process. With the current building boom in the United States, most building departments are way behind the curve. Because government agencies use taxpayers' dollars, the budget cycle and allocation for extra help and funds can take 12 to 18 months. Your local building department is no exception.

In most areas of the country, a building permit takes two weeks but can take up to four weeks. In areas experiencing the most building activity, such as southern California, Dallas–Fort Worth, Atlanta, Las Vegas, and Phoenix, a plan review, comments, resubmittal, and approvals for a building permit can take as much as two months. You need to plan ahead for the time involved in your plan review.

If you're selling the home you are currently living in or renting on a month-by-month basis, you need to account for this delay. You can have all your plans ready, the property purchased, your selects made, and the subs picked out, but you can't dig a shovel of dirt until you get your permit. If this process takes two months or more, you need to plan for that.

Government Agencies Can Take Their Time

Government agencies take their time. They are required to make sure that what you build is safe for you and safe for others. They need to make sure your new home meets all the requirements developed by your community to ensure that your home will be problem free well into the future. Checking everything necessary to review house plans takes a lot of time and involves meticulous detail.

Who Needs to Approve Your New Home Plans?

When having your new home plans reviewed by your local municipality, more than half a dozen different departments can be involved in that review process. Each department checks for different compliance, and each is there to protect you and your investment. This phase is where a qualified and experienced homebuilder comes in handy. He has the experience and understanding to know exactly what's required to get your home plans approved.

Plan Check

The plan check division is the most common compliance department and does most of the review on your new house plans. It's responsible for making sure your new home plans meet all the building codes your municipality requires.

This division makes sure your foundation is constructed to tested specifications, regulates the size and material of pipes and electrical wires, checks the exact way your fireplace and chimney are constructed, regulates the number of electrical receptacles (outlets), requires tempered glass in the shower, patio doors, or any glass lower than 3 feet, and the list goes on.

Most municipalities use a standard set of building codes as the basis for their codes. This standard set of codes is called the "International Building Code, 2004 Edition," which can be purchased at bookstores or online. The International Building Code isn't something you have to run out and purchase, however, because your homebuilder will be familiar with the specific codes for your municipality. I mention it only as a one-stop reference for any questions you might have. Most libraries carry this book, and it's available as a reference guide.

Zoning Review

The zoning review division is responsible for making sure you build the right kind of house in the right place. It's responsible for ensuring that you build your residence in an area zoned for residential construction, that the front, rear, and side setbacks adhere to its requirements, and that your home doesn't exceed the town's maximum height restrictions.

Architectural Review Board

The purpose of an architectural review board is to be sure that new construction or alterations to existing structures conform to your community's existing architectural style. An architectural review board is responsible for safeguarding and preserving the value of homes and properties within your community by ensuring that the continuity of architectural styles reflects elements of your city's cultural, social, economic, political, and architectural history.

These boards generally review new building construction, alterations to existing structures, building additions, and demolitions. Even minor changes to the exterior of a property, such as new paint or signs or removing trees and shrubs, might also be reviewed.

Whether your municipality has an architectural review board as part of its building department depends on your municipality. Many towns and cities opt not to have a board, and many others rely on the homeowner's association to police the architectural style, if one exists.

WHAT IS A HISTORIC DISTRICT?

In certain parts of the United States, historic structures might be designated as part of a historic district or designated individually. A local historic district is a group of historic resources designated for protection through zoning by your community. The ultimate goal of a local designation is to preserve the existing character of the community's neighborhoods and to maintain property values and neighborhood diversity.

All properties designated within a local historic district are subject to review by an architectural review board for any exterior changes, including demolitions. This requirement provides public notification and a review process before any changes can be made to a protected property.

Some historic properties might also be recognized as a state historic landmark and listed on the State Landmark Register or possibly as a federal landmark on the National Register of Historic Places. If your property is within a state or national historic landmark district, a list of associated restrictions makes it cost prohibitive to even build in that district. However, you might qualify for income tax credits if you do. You need to explore these restrictions with your attorney and homebuilder if they apply.

Flood Control

Flood control inspections are done by the town, city, or county you'll be building in. This agency ensures that your new home is constructed at a high enough elevation to remain safe from flooding, even under the most severe flooding conditions (usually what's referred to as a "150-year storm"). The restrictions and requirements vary depending on the municipality and even by area within a municipality. The best way to understand the specific requirements is to contact your local governing agency.

In Arizona, the center of the southwest desert, most of the Phoenix metropolitan area is considered to be located in the Salt River flood plain. The Salt River might have water for only a week at a time every few years; however, when it does flood, it can be severe. In this area, all first-floor elevations for new homes must be constructed 1 1/2 feet above the existing grade.

Flood regulations might affect how and where you build your new home. They could also add to the cost of construction if you need to bring in enough soil to raise your new home and the surrounding site by a foot and a half. So be sure to ask whether your property is in a flood plain.

Homeowner's Association

More new neighborhoods today are governed by their own homeowner's association (HOA), and many are not necessarily gated communities. These neighborhoods are sometimes referred to as *common interest developments* (*CIDs*) or *planned unit developments* (*PUDs*). According to the National Center for Policy Action (http://www.nationalcenter.org), approximately one in six people in America, or about 50 million residents, live in a community regulated by a homeowner's association. Gated HOA communities protect residents by limiting outside access to people who are "buzzed" in from the front gate and people who have been given the gate access code, which is changed periodically.

HOAs are also formed to protect the homeowner's property investment. When you visit an HOA-controlled neighborhood, you'll find that they are mostly upscale, higher-priced homes. What you won't see are brightly painted homes, RVs in the driveways, clotheslines with unmentionables, 10-foot satellite dishes, cars up on blocks, chickens running around in yards, or other things that can adversely affect the value of their homes. All this protection comes with a price.

In Chapter 7, "How to Select Property Properly," you learned that when you build a home in a new subdivision, your deed includes covenants, conditions, and restrictions (CC&Rs) that regulate (limit) how you can use your property and spell out an HOA's ability to enforce these regulations. When you purchase your home and/or property, you automatically agree to abide by every rule and regulation in the CC&Rs and become a member of your homeowner's association.

A homeowner's association is created and funded by the homeowners themselves through elections of officers and board members and the collection of mandatory monthly dues or assessments. A typical HOA's responsibilities might include the following:

- *Collect association dues*   These dues help maintain common property, including landscaping, playgrounds, pools, lakes and lakeside docks, street sweeping, jogging paths, golf courses, tennis and basketball courts, cabañas and clubhouses, streetlighting, and security.

- *Impose special assessments*   These assessments are used to finance major improvements and repairs, such as painting, gate repair, water lines, sidewalk repair, tree removal and planting, and road resurfacing.

- *Enforce the CC&Rs*   These rules include house paint colors, parking policies, and others.

- *Fine residents who break the rules*   Fines can be assessed to homeowners who break the rules with the intent to deter rule violations. These fines stay with the property and can often accrue additional fines, penalties, and interest until the rules have been complied with.

- *Foreclosure*   In rare cases, the board can foreclose on homeowners who can't afford their dues, assessments, fines, or home maintenance.

Because of the inherent power HOAs have, most town, city, and county building departments and licensing agencies won't even look at your house plans until your HOA has reviewed them and given you a letter stating that the plans meet its regulations. The building department doesn't want to review your plans until your HOA has signed off on them because too often it spends four weeks or more reviewing plans and issuing an approval, only to have the HOA find fault and make changes. If a change is made to your plans, it's back to the city, and the building department has to start its process all over again. Therefore, be sure to have your HOA approve your plans and give you a letter stating its approval before you take your house plans to the building department for a permit.

Before you purchase your new home and/or property, find out if the property you're considering has associated CC&Rs. If it does, read the document carefully, and ask to see the association's financial records. If you need help understanding them, ask your accountant or lawyer to help you. Speak with some of the residents, and ask to meet with at least one board member. Find out what problems, if any, there might be. Then you can determine whether all these rules and regulations will be compatible with your lifestyle. If you just have to raise Vietnamese pot-bellied pigs, maybe an HOA-controlled community isn't right for you.

The following table lists typical items that are controlled by homeowner's associations.

Typical HOA/CC&R Regulations

Category	Example (My CC&Rs)
Exterior paint	Preapproved colors only
Basketball hoops	None allowed
Boats	Secured to approved dock only
Cars (number and where parked)	None visible allowed
Clotheslines	None allowed
Fences	Approved block and paint

Category	Example (My CC&Rs)
Flag flying	Only on holiday with 6-foot mast
Garage sales	Neighborhood wide; four per year
Garbage cans	Out after 6 p.m.; back by 4 p.m.
Home businesses	None allowed
Lawns, landscaping	Maintenance and square footage of grass
Trees, hedges	Minimum number and approved list
Lawn mowing schedules	7 a.m. to 8 p.m.
Mailboxes	2×2×5-foot concrete pillar only
Motorbikes, motor scooters	None allowed
Noise	7 a.m. to 10 p.m.; certain types only
Open garage doors	None allowed
Outdoor lights	Approved only; no floodlights
Pets (if at all)	Number, size, and type (household)
RVs	None allowed
Sheds	No visible allowed
Signs on lawns or in windows	None allowed
TV antennas, satellite dishes	None allowed
Trailers	None allowed
Treehouses	None allowed
Obstruction of views	Bushes at lake—maximum of three feet high

Addressing

Believe it or not, the address of your new home is not assumed; your municipality must issue it. The town, city, or county where you're building your new home determines and issues your street address. You or your homebuilder should request an address early in the project because some municipalities require this information to begin the permit process.

In one instance, I completed the construction of a new home, and the homebuyers arrived from Chicago ready to move in. The day I was to get approval on their Certificate of Occupancy (C of O), the county arrived for the final inspection, and I failed. When I asked why, I was told that the county had not officially assigned the address yet. Everyone had known the address for the past six months. The home was situated between 2022 and 2026, so the address was 2024, right? It took several days before the county could assign and record the official address. As expected, it turned out to be 2024.

After I received notice that the address was officially assigned, I immediately requested my final inspection for the following morning. When I arrived at the house, the inspector told me that when he showed up at the site at 10:30 a.m., he saw that the little plastic address numbers hadn't been attached to the home yet. When I arrived at 11:00 a.m. after buying the address numbers at the hardware store, I found I had failed again.

I attached the numbers, ordered another inspection, waited another day, and finally got the C of O. You can't get final approval on your home unless it has been assigned an address and those numbers are clearly visible from the street. The reason for this requirement is fire and medical services. If there's a fire or need of an ambulance, these services need to be able to find an address easily.

This mistake on the house address cost the homebuilder four days' delay in closing on that home and four nights' hotel bills for the homebuyers, which the homebuilder reimbursed. The moral of the story is to get your street address assigned early in the process.

Summary

In this chapter, you've learned what a typical building permit submittal package includes. You've seen examples of how some municipalities calculate their costs for building permits and looked at the high cost of town and city impact fees and how they affect your budget.

This chapter has discussed the importance of your homebuilder working directly with the planning and building departments for your municipality; homebuilders can often get the job done faster and more cheaply. You've also learned how long it takes to get your building permit and why. In addition, many other departments and organizations can affect your new home and its construction, such as divisions within a building department (plan check, zoning, and architectural review), historic districts, flood control, HOAs, and addressing.

Getting your building permit is a big step in the building process. It requires a lot of preparation by your homebuilder and represents a significant line item cost in your budget. The process could take up to two months and cost as much as $16,000. This chapter has given you an overview and some examples of the process, but check with your local planning and building departments and your HOA for more detailed information, restrictions, requirements, and costs.

See "Additional Resources" on page 4 for details on how to download a free sample building permit application.

18

A Good Site Foundation Is the Base of a Good Home

Site preparation, the first step in actually building your new house, is crucial to constructing a home that will be free of foundation problems throughout the life of your new home. In this step, your homebuilder clears the site of all trees and debris, removes organic topsoil, and prepares the ground to begin building your home's foundation. Understanding the process and knowing your soils can help ensure that below it all, your home has a good foundation.

What Is Clearing and Grubbing Your Land?

Clearing and grubbing are the first steps in actually constructing your new home. *Clearing* refers to removing trees, brush, and other debris from the building site, and *grubbing* means digging out roots and other organic materials to prepare the site for your new home's foundation.

Foundation preparation, which includes clearing and grubbing, is your homebuilder's responsibility and shouldn't require your participation. The purpose of this chapter is to make you aware of the process.

Preparing Your Site for the Foundation

When your homebuilder begins to prepare the site for construction of footings, foundations, floor slabs, patios, walkways, and driveways, usually the process begins with outlining your new home's "footprint" accurately on the ground and marking trees and other obstructions within this outline for removal.

At this time, often site grading is also done outside the footprint to raise the elevation of your new home's first floor, to slope the ground away from your new home so that rainwater runs off, or maybe to grade a flat area for a septic tank, patios, a garage, outbuildings, or a driveway.

Knowing the Types of Soil That Can Affect Your Home

In the United States, you can find many different types of soil. Some can have positive effects, and others can have negative effects on the construction of your new home. Some soils are great for drainage, some are good for support, and others are poor at drainage or have too many organics and need to be removed. These soil conditions add extra costs to the construction of your new home.

Three different soil conditions can have an adverse affect on construction:

* Rock
* Cay
* Poor draining soil

Knowing the type of soil before you purchase your property can give you an indication of how much additional expense, if any, there will be to construct your new home before you're committed to that location.

Soils Can Range from Rock to Clay

Soils are made up of many types of materials of different sizes and are often a mix. Most surface soils can be categorized as *gravel*, *sand*, or *silt* including *clays* and are further classified based on the material's texture or grain size.

Soils in the United States are made up of a combination of soil types. These mixtures are commonly referred to as *loams*. The type of loam is further distinguished by its density and compaction (ability to be compressed).

The most common soil classification is *coarse-grained soils*, which consist of gravel and sand and have what's referred to as a high shear strength (good for support) and a good compaction rating. This rating means they're good soils for supporting the weight of a structure such as your new house and have good draining capabilities.

The second soil classification is *fine-grained soils*, which consist of both silt and clay and are more sensitive to moisture. Fine-grained soils, although good at compaction and supporting a structure, require moisture control to be stable as a building material. The clay materials in fine-grained soil compact solidly but are soluble and reactive in the presence of water and can undergo shrinking and swelling.

The third soil classification is clay or *super-fine-grained soils* (such as sludge). Clay is constantly moving and reacting to moisture variations in the ground, which results in shrinking (contraction) and swelling (expansion). For this reason, clay can cause what's called "differential movement," which means that one area of the home moves more or less than another area, resulting in cracks and damage to the new home.

An additional type of soil mixture is a loam containing an *organic layer*. This top layer of undisturbed soils, usually approximately 1 inch deep, contains a mix of organics, which are partially decomposed leaves, grass, branches, and other once living things. This layer of soil can't be used as

> **tip** The organic layer can, however, be used on your home site for landscaping and general grading.

a structural base for building, so it must be removed. Soils mixed with organics continue to decompose. When this decomposition takes place, the organics reduce in size, allowing the soils to collapse into the voids. If this happens under your foundation, the foundation could settle and ultimately crack.

Another condition that can cause additional expense is rock. If your building site has rock at or below the surface, your homebuilder has to excavate that rock to build the foundation and possibly the septic tank and drainage fields. Rock can also interfere with the necessary trenching for underground utilities.

> **caution** In some areas of the country, especially the Northeast, granite and schist are prevalent, and this dense rock could even require blasting to remove it. The harder rock is to remove, the more underground construction costs you.

Your homebuilder can explain the types of soils on your job site and whether he foresees any additional expenses. Just be aware of the different soil types and how they can affect the cost of site prep, and ask your homebuilder if there are any conditions that might affect construction of your new home.

Some Clays Can Move Your Foundation

Clay soils are everywhere throughout the United States and can create two potential problems: *drainage* and *expansion*. If there's clay in your home site, you could encounter problems with the soil draining runoff rainwater away from the foundation and draining the septic system, if you have one. Expanding clay can also create problems by raising your home and cracking the foundation, creating the differential movement explained previously. Clay is a very fine mineral, part of the larger class of silicate minerals called phyllosilicates. Included in the phyllosilicate family are the larger true micas, which include the minerals muscovite and biotite. What do these terms mean for you?

If your home site soils contain a high quantity of some types of clays, you could have a situation with poor drainage, which can affect your septic fields and rainwater runoff. Clay of the expansive type can expand as much as 60% in volume. Vermiculite and kitty litter are two common examples of expanding clay. The most common expansive clay found on U.S. building sites is betonite. This tight, fine-particle clay can shrink at an average rate of 3/4 inch per cubic foot. The depth of this clay can range from 2 feet to approximately 15 feet from the surface. The amount of expansion and contraction depends on the amount of water in the soil. Some areas of the country have large amounts of betonite in the soil, which can cause damage to already constructed homes, prohibit the construction of new homes, or, at the very least, change the way some homes are constructed.

THE DENVER FLOATING WALL

In and around Denver, Colorado, are high concentrations of betonite. During unusually wet periods, the betonite clay beneath homes has swelled enough to raise houses up off their foundations. To help prevent this from happening, homebuilders have created the Denver Floating Wall.

Using the Denver Floating Wall technique, the homebuilder constructs walls in the basement 3 inches short of touching the basement floor, and then anchors the walls to the first floor above. A wider baseboard is installed to cover this wall-to-floor gap. When the betonite gets wet and begins to swell and lift the basement floor up, the floor simply rises to meet the hanging wall. This prevents the floor from pushing the wall up against the first-floor joists and raising the house off the foundation.

How often does the problem of expansive clay happen? Rarely, but it does. Recently in the north Phoenix metropolitan area of Anthem, this condition has affected six new homes to date.

To prevent this problem, ask your homebuilder if he's had a soil test done to check for the percentage of betonite clay in the soil. Doing this test is in his best interest as well because he's responsible for any differential settling and subsequent damage for up to the next two years.

Why Soil Compaction Is Important

Soil compaction is important because you want to be sure your new home is on a solid subsurface that won't settle or move over the next 50 years or more. If your whole house settled equally, you would never know it. It's differential settling (movement) that causes a problem.

During *differential settling*, one area under your home settles more than another. When this happens, the foundation might crack, and you might also see cracking in patios, driveways, stucco walls, and interior drywall. Usually, these cracks are purely cosmetic and cause no real damage to your new home. If these cracks do occur, contact your homebuilder and have him inspect as soon as he can and, if necessary, make the cosmetic repairs. If the cracking becomes a larger problem, he'll know and take the appropriate steps to prevent it in the future.

To prevent differential settling, your homebuilder and his excavator take great care to ensure that your subsurface soils are the right type, are free of organic materials, and are compacted properly. *Compaction* is done by adding layer after layer of good soils, sprinkling them with water, and rolling over them with heavy machinery. This rolling can be done with a machine designed specifically to roll and compact surfaces, which is called a "roller," or simply by driving a large bucket loader or bulldozer repeatedly over the surface.

Understand Soil and Compaction Reports

After your building site has been compacted, your homebuilder is required to have a soil-engineering test performed. For this test, an engineer bores into the soil with an auger in three or more places, removes the soil from those spots, and determines the percentage of compaction in those soils.

After this test is done, the soils engineer gives your builder a certificate of compaction that states the percentage of compaction he found on your building site. The compaction rate must be at least 95% or higher.

Your homebuilder is responsible for having this test done and for obtaining the certificate. Any time you want to see this certificate, just ask your homebuilder to give you a copy.

Summary

This chapter has explained what it means to clear and grub your home site and how your homebuilder prepares the site by removing any obstructions and organics. You learned about the different soil types and how they could affect construction costs for your new home. Betonite clay, for example, can damage your new home by expanding and contracting up to 60%, so it's important to make sure your homebuilder tests for the presence of this expansive clay. Again, with a good excavator and foundation subcontractor, this problem doesn't happen often, but when it does, it can cause anything from minor cracks in the foundation to something much more serious.

You also learned why soil compaction is important to keeping your new home on the level. Asking your homebuilder for a copy of the compaction certificate is a wise idea.

The best prevention against possible increased construction costs and potential damage to your new home is to research the soils on your property before you purchase it. If the land comes with your new home, discuss the type of soils on your property with your homebuilder and realtor to see whether these soils could pose a problem for your new home construction.

See "Additional Resources" on page 4 for details on how to download a free sample soil compaction report.

19

Getting the Jump on Termites Before You Start

This chapter is about termites, how they affect you, and how you and your home-builder can keep them from eating you out of house and home. Even though they can cause a great deal of damage, termites can be prevented with some simple routine maintenance and planning.

Why Termites Can Be a Serious Problem

The following are a few facts about termites:

- Termites cause more than $5 billion in damage to homes each year in the United States. That's more damage than fire, earthquake, and other weather-related damage combined!

- Termites thrive in 49 of the 50 U.S. states.

- Termites number more than 40 different species in the United States and 2,000 species worldwide.

- Termite workers eat through plaster, plastic, and even asphalt to get to a wood food source and can travel up to 250 feet away from the colony.

- Termites infest 1 of every 30 U.S. homes each year, totaling more than 50 billion termites.
- A small colony of approximately 60,000 termites can eat one linear foot of 2×4-inch lumber every five months.
- Termites never sleep; they work 24 hours a day.
- One acre of land can contain more than one million termites.

The focus of this book is on new home construction where existing termite infestation is not an issue; however, termite prevention is a required step in building your new home. In this chapter, I include material describing termites, explaining how to detect them, and explaining how to prevent them after you take ownership of your new home because keeping your home free of termites from the start is important.

What Are Termites?

The most common termite in the United States is the *subterranean termite*. Termites feed on cellulose, which comes from dead wood, leaves, mulch, paper, and other wood products. Subterranean termites live below the surface of the soil, where they excavate tunnels extending up to several hundred feet to reach water and food. Termites need both cellulose and moisture to survive. Subterranean termites live in colonies that can contain hundreds of thousands of termites.

The common scientific name for the subterranean termite is *Reticulitermes flavipes*. Each termite colony contains three types or castes of termites: workers, soldiers, and reproductives.

Workers are about 1/8 inch long, blind, wingless, soft-bodied, creamy white to grayish white with a round head. Workers are the most numerous termites and the ones that actually eat wood. Worker termites are sterile, forage for food and water, construct and repair the colony's shelter tubes, feed and groom the other termites, care for eggs and the young, and defend the colony.

Soldier termites are also wingless and resemble workers except they have a large rectangular yellowish brown head with large mandibles (jaws). The soldier termite's primary responsibility is defending the colony.

Last are the male and female *reproductives*. They can be winged (mostly) or wingless. Winged termite reproductives are also called *alates* or *swarmers*. Swarmers shed their wings soon after their flight. Their body color varies by species from black to yellowish brown, and they are about 0.4 inch long, with pale or grayish translucent wings. A pair of reproductives heading a colony is called the king and queen.

How Do You Detect Termites?

Being able to recognize the signs of a subterranean termite infestation is important. Subterranean termites can be detected by the sudden emergence of winged termites (alates or swarmers) or by the presence of mud tubes around your foundation and wood damage in the form of visible tunnels and honeycombs.

Winged termites swarm in large numbers from wood or the ground. Swarming occurs in mature colonies that typically contain at least several thousand termites. A swarm is made up of adult male and female reproductives, which leave their colony in an attempt to pair up and begin new colonies. Although a colony can have many reproductives, only two successfully pair up as king and queen.

These emergences are stimulated when temperature and moisture conditions are favorable, usually on warm days following rainfall. Swarming typically occurs during the daytime in the spring but can occur indoors during other months. Swarming usually occurs during a brief period, usually less than an hour, and swarmers shed their wings quickly. The presence of winged termites or shed wings inside a home is a warning of termite infestation.

Other signs of termites are mud tubes and lumps of mud protruding from cracks in your home's wood. Subterranean termites use soil and water to construct tunnels called shelter tubes above ground, which allow them to navigate exposed areas to reach food and water. Shelter tubes, which are usually 1/4 to 1 inch wide, protect them from drying out and from predators, such as ants. To determine whether there's an active colony, scrape away the shelter tubes and then monitor the area to see if termites construct new tubes.

Termite damage to wood is often not obvious because termites chew their way through wood as they feed. Wood damaged by termite infestation has a honey-combed appearance, and these honeycombs are often packed with soil and waste. When you tap the wood, it has a hollow sound. Subterranean termites don't reduce wood to a powder or create wood particles or pellets, as many other wood-boring insects do.

Pretreat to Prevent Insects Before You Begin Building

More homes in the United States are being built on undeveloped land or land previously used for agriculture. The more new homes are built on these types of land, the greater the opportunity for conflict between man and termite—and even more reason for pretreatment to prevent termite infestation. Over the past several years, there have been many changes in the type of products that can be used, the methods of applying these products, and the amount of regulation required for termite pretreatment.

Subterranean termite pretreatment is a preventive measure. A licensed pest control company sprays an oily liquid *termiticide* (a pesticide specifically for termites) onto the soil where the foundation will be constructed and on the surrounding area of a residential dwelling. Spraying these areas creates a barrier to prevent subterranean termites from being able to access your new home. Termite pretreatment is applied directly to the soil and acts a continuous chemical barrier beneath the foundation. This liquid barrier is designed to be toxic or repellent to termites coming in contact with it. Termites can circumvent the chemical treatment if there are untreated gaps in the soil, however. These treatments can require more than 100 gallons of termiticide, depending on the size of your new house.

Termiticides that act by creating a chemical barrier in the soil include bifenthrin (Talstar), cypermethrin (Demon, Prevail), and permethrin (Dragnet, Prelude). The most recent termiticides on the market, however, are nonrepellent. These chemicals have a delayed toxicity, so termites don't avoid treated soil as they forage through it. As termites penetrate the treated zone, they contact the active ingredient, which causes a delayed death. The toxin is passed to other termites in the colony through grooming and food exchange (trophallaxis). After a colony has become exposed to these chemicals, it's usually destroyed within three months. Nonrepellent termiticides include fipronil (Termidor), imidacloprid (Premise), and chlorfenapyr (Phantom).

For termite pretreatment to be effective, a final application of termiticide must be sprayed after the final grading is done and landscaping is completed. Generally, these pretreatments have a warranty for five years and sometimes up to 10 years for newer termiticides, such as Termidors.

Termite pretreatment is an effective way of preventing termites from tunneling under your new home's foundation and finding their way in. However, this barrier is successful only if you have a pest control company retreat areas when you make improvements or repairs that require breaking or cutting into the concrete slab or digging into soil that touches the outside foundation. Using the pest control company that originally treated and guaranteed your home during construction is the best way to maintain the integrity of your new home and ensure your warranty. If you build any concrete patios, room additions, garages, or carports or make any other alterations that disturb the soil, these areas need to be treated again. If you don't treat these areas, you could void your original pretreatment warranty and run the risk of termite infestation.

The Federal Housing Administration (FHA), Veterans Administration Department of Housing and Urban Development (VA HUD), and laws in many communities require termite pretreatment. These laws specify that any building constructed as a single-family residence that could be sold with FHA or VA HUD financing must have termite soil pretreatment.

The pest control company is responsible for retreatment during the applicable warranty period. The FHA/VA HUD warranty states that the builder agrees to repair all construction damage within the one-year homebuilder's warranty period. Generally, the homeowner is responsible for repairing termite damage after the homebuilder's warranty has expired.

Other Forms of Pretreatment Help Keep Your Home Safe

You and your homebuilder can take other first-step preventive measures in protecting your new home from termites. Whenever wood is in direct contact with soil or exposed to moisture, using pressure-treated wood is advisable. Wood treated with borates (disodium octaborate tetrahydrate, such as Tim-bor, Bora-Care, Jecta, and Impel) and pressure treatments (creosote, chromated copper arsenate [CCA]) protect wood against termites. Be aware, however, that creosote-treated railroad ties and telephone poles and other CCA-treated wood can, over time, be subject to termite attack. Also, as of January 1, 2004, CCA-treated wood is no longer available for use in residential construction because of concerns about its arsenic levels.

For older wood, untreated wood, and pressure-treated wood that has been cut, you can apply borates, which don't contain arsenic, with a paintbrush. As an alternative to pressure-treated wood, you can use natural termite-resistant woods, such as redwood, cedar, and juniper.

Physical barriers are easy to set up during preconstruction of your new home. One type of physical barrier is a stainless-steel wire mesh (TermiMesh) that can be fitted around pipes, posts, or foundations. The newest physical barrier, Impasse Termite System, contains a liquid termiticide (lambda-cyhalothrin) sealed between two layers of a heavy plastic that's installed before the concrete slab is poured. It's supplemented with Impasse Termite Blocker, which uses special fittings around plumbing and electrical pipe and conduit foundation penetrations.

Metal termite shields called Mermite have been used for decades to deter termite movement along foundation walls and piers. These shields work well if they're installed properly and don't become damaged or deteriorated, which could allow termites to penetrate your new home. These shields should be made of noncorroding metal, have no cracks or gaps along seams where sections are attached, and extend at least 2 inches out and 2 inches down at a 45-degree angle from the foundation wall.

You can also use "termite-resistant" siding materials. A number of building materials are becoming more popular as alternatives to conventional siding, which are typically vulnerable to termites. These new products, which include HardiPlank and HardiPanel, are termite (and decay) resistant and usually carry a long-term limited warranty. Keep in mind that these products are more expensive than conventional building materials.

Tests have shown that even sand and gravel can be used. A layer of sand with uniform size particles (roughly 16-grit) is placed along the foundation to a depth of at least 4 inches and trailing outward to about 20 inches. You can also use stone or Granitgard, which consists of finely graded stone particles. This stone is laid beneath concrete floors of new buildings or around foundations. With sand and stone, the particles are too closely packed to navigate through or build stable tunnels or are too large for termites to move with their mandibles.

> **caution** Landscaping should not be installed within 16 inches of your new foundation, and irrigation should be installed outside the plant line. Avoid installing fence posts, trellises, or any other wooden decor that might touch both the ground and your home.

The Pretreatment Certificate and Warranty

When your new home is pretreated for termites during the course of construction, the pest control company gives your homebuilder a pretreatment certificate and a warranty, which are yours to keep. They show you the terms of your warranty and list the company's name and contact information. This information is helpful if you disturb the soils around the foundation and need additional treatment or in the unlikely event of termite infestation. Be sure to ask for your pretreatment certificate and warranty from your homebuilder.

How You Can Help Prevent Termites After Construction

As Benjamin Franklin said, "An ounce of prevention is worth a pound of cure." When it comes to termites, no truer words were spoken. A little common sense can go a long way toward preventing termite damage to your new home. Termite prevention is easy and effective; it's all about disrupting termites' ability to gain access to your home for food (wood), moisture, and shelter.

Some Simple Measures Can Keep You Termite Free

Here are a few precautions you can take to protect your new home from termite infestation:

- Don't allow water to accumulate near the foundation. Water is a key ingredient for termite survival. Divert surface water away from your foundation with downspouts, gutters, splash blocks, and soil that's graded or sloped away from your foundation to drain properly.
- Remove cellulose (wood, mulch, paper, and so forth). Cellulose, termites' food source, is the second key ingredient for their survival. Eliminate any contact

between wooden parts of your house and the soil, and maintain at least 6 inches between wood and soil. Contact between wood and soil is how termites gain access to your home and their food. Wooden parts of a house can include steps, latticework, door or window frames, siding, posts, fences, and so on.

- Never stack or store firewood, lumber, newspapers, fence posts, landscaping or railroad ties, or other wood products against the foundation.

- During construction, never bury wood scraps, waste lumber, or other wood products near the foundation. This food source will attract termite colonies.

- Remove wooden or cellotex form boards, grade stakes, or other wood used during construction. Avoid or minimize use of wood mulch next to your foundation. If you do use mulch, be sure to allow a 6-inch gap between the mulch and the siding to prevent termites from tunneling up the foundation and getting into your home.

- Lay a minimum of 6mm polyethylene plastic in crawlspaces under foundations as a moisture barrier between the soil and the subfloor.

- Keep crawlspaces as dry as possible.

- Prune back plants, trees, and hedges that are close to your home to prevent moisture and mold buildup.

- Adjust sprinklers to keep them from spraying directly onto your walls and siding.

- Seal all exposed wood against moisture with a good weather sealer.

Summary

This chapter has explained how to identify signs of termite infestation and how termites can affect your new home. Being able to detect termites before they cause damage is important.

Termite pretreatment is essential, and you've learned how it's done and the importance of getting the pretreatment certificate and warranty from your homebuilder. You can also build termite treatment into your new home and take preventive measures to keep your home safe after it's finished.

See "Additional Resources" on page 4 for details on how to download a free sample termite inspection report.

20

What You Need to Know About Your New Septic System

This chapter may or may not apply to the construction of your new home. Most new homes today are connected to a city wastewater facility; however, with housing developments and new home construction moving farther out into rural areas, septic systems can be an issue for new homebuyers. If you find that you're going to be the proud owner of a new septic system, this chapter is designed for you.

How Does a Septic System Work?

The average water consumption in U.S. homes today is approximately 8 gallons per person. This average includes toilet flushes and a category of water wastewater called "gray water," which can be water from showers, baths, the dishwasher, the washer, and the kitchen sink. All this wastewater can add up. A family of five uses 40 gallons of water per day. This equals roughly 1,200 gallons per month or close to 15,000 gallons of wastewater per year.

The most common onsite residential wastewater treatment system is called a *septic system*. This system is very low tech: It consists of a tank and a leach well or leach fields. A rectangular septic tank, about the size of a standard SUV, is connected to the house, with the connection buried in your backyard. The septic tank, made from steel-reinforced concrete, captures all the water and other wastes and separates water from solids.

Solid wastes and other materials settle to the bottom of the tank as sludge, grease floats to the top as scum, and liquid flows out of the tank through a pipe into the leach well or leach fields as what's called *liquid effluent*. The solids and sludge that remain in the tank are eaten or slowly digested by anaerobic bacteria.

> **note** Anaerobic bacteria live without the presence of oxygen. ("Anaerobic" is the opposite of "aerobic.")

A leach well is nothing more than a vertical hole, usually 6 feet in diameter and 20 or so feet deep, filled with coarse gravel; however, the most common leaching system is leach fields. To create leach fields, a series of trenches are dug in the backyard just below the frost line (3 feet in most areas). These trenches are filled with gravel and perforated pipes, and then covered with landscaping material to prevent soil from filling up the pipes. Leach pipes fill with the overflow liquid effluent, and the perforations or holes in the bottom of the pipe simply allow the liquid to "leach" into the ground. Believe it or not, that's all there is to a septic system.

DO I EVEN NEED A SEPTIC SYSTEM?

One way or another, you need to address wastewater in your new home. If your home will be connected to a city wastewater or sewer system or your city sewer district, all your homebuilder needs to do is secure a permit to connect to it, trench and install your sewer drain pipe to the street, and excavate the street to connect your new pipe to the city's pipe. If you're not in an area where you can connect, your wastewater is your responsibility. This is where a septic system comes in.

How Does a Perk Test Affect the System Cost?

Before a homebuilder can sell property to you, he or an engineer must perform a perk test. A *perk test* (short for percolation test) determines how big your leach well or leach fields need to be for your family's 1,200+ gallons of water to penetrate (percolate) into the soil each month. A perk test measures how fast water leaches or seeps into your particular soil.

Your soil type also determines how big leach fields need to be. The more clay or "fines" (fine-grained soils, as discussed in Chapter 18, "A Good Site Foundation Is the Base of a Good Home") are in your soil, the harder it is for water to penetrate into the ground. The slower water leaches, the bigger the fields need to be or the more linear feet of perforated pipe you need to get a constant flow of effluent into the ground.

Good Soils Can Make Your Septic System Less Expensive

If the soils on your building site are a good mixture of coarse- and fine-grained soils, the more efficiently wastewater leaches into the soil. The more fine-grained the soil is, the more slowly wastewater leaches into the soil. Soils that are a good mixture of coarse- and fine-grained soils are often referred to as *sandy loam*. The faster the absorption, the less pipe, trenching, gravel, landscape material, and labor you need to construct the septic system.

What Happens During a Perk Test?

A perk test is a fairly easy process. An engineer goes to your building site and locates the approximate spot where the septic system will be installed, usually in the backyard about 20 or so feet from the house.

Using a posthole digger, he digs a hole 1 foot in diameter and 3 feet deep. He then fills this hole to the top with water and waits one hour. At the end of that hour, he measures the distance from the bottom of the hole to the top of the water level. That's how many inches of water or percolation your soil allows. He then goes back to his office, consults his engineering book for the number of gallons of wastewater your type of house generates per day, cross-references this amount to the inches per hour, and voilà—that's how many feet of perforated pipe the septic system needs.

Speak with Your Homebuilder About Septic Costs at the Start

Before your homebuilder sells property to you, he has already performed a perk test, calculated the septic system's design, and figured the cost. There should be no surprises for you or him. The cost of building your septic system should be included in the total cost of your new home.

If your soil is average for your area, your homebuilder knows off the top of his head the cost for your septic system. The cost should be fixed and included. There should be additional expenses only if, while installing your septic system, your homebuilder hits rock or encounters other unforeseen obstacles, such as underground utilities, wells, or old septic tanks that need to be removed. Speak with your homebuilder to see whether he thinks any unforeseen additional expenses associated with building the septic system are possible.

If any additional expenses are incurred, they should be covered in a "not to exceed" clause in the contract with your homebuilder; this clause allows him to charge you an additional fixed amount. If he hasn't provided for additional septic system costs, the costs should be fixed, with no additional expense to you.

To do list

- ❑ Start up your new system with a septic system starter kit from your home warehouse store.
- ❑ Be sure your septic fields are graded to reduce water accumulation.
- ❑ Pump your tank at least every five years.
- ❑ Save the tank cover location plan your homebuilder gives you.
- ❑ Don't put anything into your system that isn't biodegradable.
- ❑ Don't put anything poisonous into your system that kills the anaerobic bacteria.

Maintaining a Happy Relationship with Your Septic System

The key to a septic system is maintaining a healthy septic system. I know this sounds repetitive, but a septic system filled with healthy anaerobic bacteria means low maintenance and efficient digestion of solids and wastes. When your septic system is healthy, what you put into the septic system stays in the septic system in your backyard—where it belongs.

As the heart of your septic system is bacteria, and it's important to keep them happy and healthy. This is why you should never put anything down your sinks or toilets that isn't biodegradable or anything that is toxic to bacteria. Items that aren't biodegradable either get stuck in the pipes or just sit forever in the tank. Poisonous materials, such as paint, paint thinner, gasoline, bleach, motor oil, and other chemicals, kill anaerobic bacteria and slow or stop the digestion or decomposition of solids. If the tank fills up with solids, it will back up, and you know what that means.

Another word of caution is to keep excess rainwater from collecting over the leach fields. Because this water also needs to be absorbed in the same area as your septic system, excess rainwater could overburden your soil and render the leach fields inoperable. To prevent this from happening, just grade the surface to encourage runoff to flow away or around your leach fields.

When you move into your new home, your septic system is also new and unused. To kick-start the digestion process, you need to kick-start the anaerobic bacteria. This task is simple. Just visit your local home warehouse or

> **tip** You can also use a cake of baker's yeast, but the hardware store version is cheaper.

hardware store, and ask the salesclerk for a septic system starter kit. This kit is a container of anaerobic bacteria, the kind you need for the system to work properly. Just pour the stuff into a toilet and flush it. That's it.

KEEP YOUR SEPTIC TANK COVER LOCATION PLAN

Your homebuilder will give you a septic tank cover location plan, which is a simple diagram that shows dimensions from two corners of your house. When you measure those lengths, they cross at only one exact point, the center of your septic tank cover. If you lose this diagram, you might have to dig up large areas of your backyard to locate the septic tank cover.

With occasional pumping and proper care and feeding of your new septic system, it can last for 50 years or more with little or no maintenance necessary.

Summary

This chapter has discussed whether you will need a septic system. You have also learned how a septic system works and how it's designed.

This chapter has also explained what a perk test is and discussed factors that might affect the cost of a septic system. Finally, you learned how to keep a septic system running efficiently so that you and your septic system can have a happy relationship for many years to come.

See "Additional Resources" on page 4 for details on how to download a free sample septic system permit.

21

What You Can Find When Doing a Home Inspection

Home inspections can buy you a great deal of peace of mind when closing on your new home. For only a few hundred dollars, you can know that your home is as close to perfect as possible, or you'll have documented what isn't right. This knowledge helps you determine what items need to be corrected before your take possession of your new home. Having a home inspection report done can also help when developing your final "punch list" for your homebuilder to correct.

Is a Home Inspection of a New Home Important?

A home inspection is a topic that causes a lot of controversy in my classes. My opinion is that it's best to wait until just before you take possession before having a home inspection done. Now, I also have to inform you that if you take this advice and something goes wrong, I can't assume any liability. Based on my personal experiences, inspections during the course of construction slow and often stop construction until every item in the report has been verified.

For several years, I was a residential home inspector, and it was my job to find things wrong or in question. That's what I got paid for. If I submitted a report to a homebuyer that stated "Everything looks good to me! Here's my bill for $350," the homebuyer might be reluctant to write a check for that. I would use terminology such as "In my opinion," "There's a possibility that," or "I would recommend." This wording is designed to provide a caution about potential problems reduce my liability, and appear to add value to the report by pointing out potential problems.

Once a homebuyer had an inspection of her home done without notifying me, the superintendent, first. The inspector inspected the home just before the drywall installation, at about the 50% completion milestone. It was more than a month before the homebuyer informed me that the report had been issued and stated "In my opinion, there may have been inadequate strapping installed between the roof trusses and the walls." The homebuyer was upset and scared that the roof was going to fall in on her and her family.

By that point, all the trusses, strapping, and walls were completely covered with drywall. To "prove" there was adequate strapping installed, the homebuilder would have had to rip out the walls and ceilings throughout the house at a cost of approximately $10,000 and three to four weeks' delay.

I assured the homebuyer that I had inspected the home personally, the homebuilder had inspected it, the framing foreman had inspected it, the owner of the framing company had inspected it, and the county inspector had inspected it and issued a certificate of completion and compliance.

The project stopped for more than a month while the homebuyer and homebuilder for whom I was the superintendent decided what to do. The final decision was to proceed with the construction, with the homebuyer trusting that everyone had inspected and approved the strapping.

These types of delays are common when the home is inspected before it's finished. This is not to say that some errors couldn't be found if an early inspection is done; it's more about the problems it can cause. I recommend waiting until the project is completed and coordinating the inspection with your homebuilder.

Who's Been Inspecting Your New Home Already?

During construction, your new home can go through dozens of official and unofficial inspections and at least eight different official government inspections, which can include everything from flood control, electrical and plumbing rough-in, footing and slab, and framing to strapping and shearing, mechanical, drywall nail, final flood control inspection, and final inspection.

Inspections are carried out by your homebuilder; his superintendent; the foreman for each trade (such as framing, plumbing, and electrical work); the owners of each subcontractor company; the city, town, or county; Occupational Safety and Health Administration (OSHA); environmental agencies; the septic inspector; electric and telephone company field foremen; water and sewer departments; building and planning departments; the bank, mortgage company, and lending institution (or appointee); you; and your friends, family, and new neighbors. Subcontractors, their foremen, and their company owners inspect for liability reasons, government agencies inspect for permit and licensing reasons, and your friends and family inspect for fun. That's okay. You want that many people watching the progress of your new home to be sure it's being constructed properly.

Even with all of these inspections, about 15% of the nearly 2 million new homes constructed this year in the United States will have at least one construction defect that requires repair.

Should I Do a Prepossession Inspection?

A *prepossession inspection* of your new home, done just before you take ownership and coordinated with your homebuilder, is a good idea. Hiring a qualified home inspector is the best way to discover whether your new home has some not-so-obvious problems. Most professional inspectors have a background in construction, engineering, architecture, or contracting and can recognize potential problems. Their responsibility is to inspect every square inch of your new home to identify and document problems or shortcomings. The home inspector gives you a report and photographs that outline potential and real problems he found, describes their impact, and makes

note You can find home inspectors by looking in the yellow pages, visiting http://www.switchboard.com, or contacting the American Society of Home Inspectors (ASHI) at http://www.ashi.com, which has approximately 1,400 member inspectors nationally. You can also go to InspectAmerica Home Inspections at http://www.inspectamerica.com for more information on home inspectors.

recommendations for fixing them. This report can be used as a *punch list* (a list of remaining items to be repaired or corrected) for your homebuilder to work with his subcontractors on making the necessary repairs. The fee for this service usually runs between $300 and $500 but could cost more.

Is a Home Warranty Necessary for My New Home?

Whether a home warranty is necessary depends on the type, extent, and term of warranty your new homebuilder provides as part of the contract price for your new home. Ask for a copy of your warranty, and discuss its terms before you sign the agreement with your homebuilder. Understand and discuss what's covered and what isn't, who will make repairs, what those repairs will cost you (if anything), how long these items will be covered, and what happens if your homebuilder goes out of business.

You can purchase home warranty insurance policies to supplement what your homebuilder provides and for use when your homebuilder's warranty (or he) runs out. The cost of these policies can start at $350 and run to around $500 or more, depending on your deductible and what items are covered.

Is the Homebuilder Responsible for the Warranty of My New Home?

The law doesn't require homebuilders to provide new home warranties; however, most reputable homebuilders do provide them. These warranties are usually limited and provide warranty against poor workmanship and material defects for one year. Many large national homebuilding companies offer a 10-year limited warranty. Under these warranties, the homebuilder is obligated to repair any defective item after the homeowner has contacted him in writing.

When you take possession of your new home, be sure to get a signed warranty at the time you receive your closing package with all the product warranties offered by manufacturers of your home's materials. If something does go wrong with materials or appliances in your new home, you're instructed to contact the manufacturer or subcontractor, not the homebuilder, for these repairs.

Some homebuilders offer an extended new-house warranty called an "insured warranty." This warranty generally covers any systems, such as plumbing and electrical, for a 2- to 10-year period. It might also warranty the structure for up to 10 years. Insured warranties are actually issued by an insurance company, which means your home is covered even if the homebuilder goes out of business.

Ten Things You Can Inspect

Here are 10 things you can inspect yourself before taking possession:

- *Structure*   Step back as far as you can and determine whether the walls appear to be straight, plumb, and flat. Are any walls bowed or not square at the corners? Jump up and down in the middle of each room. Does your floor flex or squeak? Does it feel solid?

- *Water runoff*   Does the ground slope away from the foundation of your house? Will gutters, downspouts, and other drainage pipes carry rainwater away from your house properly?

- *Roof*   Does it look neat and seem installed correctly? Is there any staining on inside ceilings from leaks? Are there any cracked or missing roof tiles or shingles?

- *Details*   Do you see any signs of poor workmanship in the finish details, such as moldings, tile work, cabinetry, drywall, hardware, caulking, carpet, weather stripping, or paint?

- *Plumbing*   Are sinks, toilets, and tubs quality fixtures, and do they work properly? Is the water pressure good when you turn on the faucets and flush the toilet at the same time? Does the water get hot when it runs in each faucet? Do any drains leak under the cabinets?

- *Electrical*   Are the number and locations of receptacles adequate? Does every one of the receptacles work? Is the main electrical service at least 100 amps? Are all circuit breakers marked to indicate what they control?

- *Water heater*   Are the water heater pipes copper? Are they insulated? Does your water tank have earthquake strapping? If it's gas, is it vented properly? Can you access the water heater tank drain easily?

- *Heating and air conditioning*   Are the furnace, heater, and AC unit accessible? Are any rooms not heated or cooled enough? Do register sizes look adequate for heating rooms? Is the return air filter easily accessible for changing and cleaning?

- *Insulation*   Does the attic have at least 6 inches of R-19 insulation in moderate climates and 12 inches of R-38 insulation in cold climates? If you remove an electric receptacle cover on an exterior wall, is there wall insulation?

- *Fireplaces*   Does your fireplace have a screen (or glass doors, which are more efficient)? Do the damper, log lighter, and/or gas insert function properly? Is there a combustion vent that draws air from the outside? Is there a spark arrester or critter stop at the top of your chimney?

Summary

This chapter has discussed why you might want to wait until your home is finished to have a home inspection done and explained how an inspection report could cost you time and money. You have also learned about all the different inspections your house undergoes during the course of construction.

You've learned about the importance of reading your new home warranty to find out what's covered and what isn't. In addition, you now have a list of 10 things you can inspect yourself before you take possession of your new home.

See "Additional Resources" on page 4 for details on how to download a free sample home inspection report.

What to Look for Before You Take Possession

22

Taking possession of your new home is one of the last steps in the process of building your new house. At this stage, you and your homebuilder walk through the house and agree that everything is as it should be or make a punch list of things that aren't. You also get your homeowner's manuals, and your homebuilder explains how all the features in your new home work. Finally, you agree to take ownership of your new home and pay your homebuilder the final payment. Then you move in and begin enjoying your new home!

In this chapter:

* Learn what's involved in taking possession of your new home

* Understand how your new home will age over the first year

* See what you need to do at the time of closing

* Explore why your home-builder's walkthrough is so important

To do list

- ☐ Perform the walkthrough with your homebuilder.
- ☐ Get a "checklist" from your homebuilder or from http://www.BetterHomesSeminars.com.
- ☐ Create a punch List and have your homebuilder agree to and sign it.
- ☐ Get your homeowner's manuals, care instructions for your new home, and contact list from your homebuilder.

What Happens at the Walkthrough

After your new home passes final inspection by all the necessary government agencies, your homebuilder calls you to set up a homeowner's walkthrough. The purpose of the walkthrough is to give you the opportunity to ask any questions you might have about the construction of your new home. It also provides for a cooperative inspection of the finished home. (The most efficient way to handle the walkthrough inspection is to use a checklist. I talk about this topic in more detail in the "A Walkthrough Checklist Can Ensure You Look at Everything" section later in this chapter.) Any items in your new home that aren't completed correctly or as you wanted can be added to a *punch list*. The appropriate subcontractors can then schedule punch list items for repair.

note The homeowner's walkthrough is for the principal buyers only. The homebuilder often asks that additional family members, brokers, realtors, or friends not accompany you on the walkthrough. The reason for this request is so that he can give you the personal attention and time needed to familiarize you with your new home without the distraction of a large group.

Before your walkthrough of your new home, your homebuilder asks you to make arrangements to have the power and water turned on in the home in your name.

The homebuilder is responsible for any damages and defective materials or workmanship. The homebuilder is not responsible for manufactured items included in the home, such as appliances. They are warranted by the manufacturer and usually aren't included in his warranty. In most cases, it's the owner's responsibility to file any warranty cards to ensure valid manufacturers' warranties.

Materials used in your new home are subject to some degree of slight imperfection or damage through handling and installation. Minor variations in wood finishes, tile coloration, and paint pigment and minor, hard-to-see nicks, scratches, cuts, blemishes, finish variations, and other similar natural variations in products can occur to some degree and aren't considered construction defects. If these defects are readily apparent and are considerable, you should discuss having your homebuilder fix them at this time. Further, imperfections in workmanship or materials of finished products don't warrant repair if they aren't visible with the naked eye in natural or artificial light from a distance of six feet.

Early Effects of Your Home Stabilizing

Many items in a new home might cause you concern but are normal in the early aging (also referred to as "stabilizing") of your new home. Here are some items you might notice that are normal and shouldn't be of concern:

- *Concrete*   In the process of curing, concrete shrinks, so cracks are normal. If they become too wide, your homebuilder should repair them. "Too wide" can be defined by the thickness of a nickel. If you can place a nickel standing on its end into a crack, report it to your homebuilder. Control cuts or control joints are straight cuts in the concrete that are covered by your home's flooring (except in the garage and on walkways and patios) and aren't visible in your finished home. These cuts and joints are put in the concrete to help control the natural "cracking" by allowing the crack to follow the joint in a straight, controlled line and shouldn't cause concern.

- *Stucco*   The stucco on the exterior of your new home is also a concrete-based product and over the course of any year is exposed to extreme temperatures, ranging from below freezing to above 100 degrees (F) in summer heat. Cracks *will* appear. The homebuilder should repair any cracks at least once during the one-year warranty period or at the end of that period. I recommend waiting for your new home to go through a full summer and winter (or waiting until just before the expiration of your one-year warranty) before having cracks repaired.

- *Hard floors*   Many homebuyers choose a "hard" floor finish, such as tile or stone, in certain areas of their home. Be aware that this type of flooring doesn't deaden sound; it actually reflects sounds. So the larger the area you cover in hard finishes, the noisier your house could be. This type of flooring can also be easily damaged by dropping items such as frying pans and by moving heavy appliances, furniture, pianos, and so forth. It can also crack because of shrinking concrete. Therefore, this type of flooring usually has a limited warranty. The larger the area, the more likely you are to have cracking and shrinkage.

It's normal for all new homes to go through a period of minor adjustment or a stabilization period, so living in your home for at least 60 to 90 days before you begin compiling a list of needed cosmetic repairs is advisable. Generally, you should send this list via certified U.S. mail or fax it to your homebuilder 30 days before the end of the warranty period. This allows your home-builder to do a complete and thorough job the first time around instead of in bits and pieces, which becomes a nuisance to you, your home-builder, and subcontractors.

caution You need to be aware that if your home is damaged by acts of nature after the close of escrow, the repairs aren't be covered under warranties. The repairs then become your responsibility and that of your homeowner's insurance company.

Homeowner's Insurance and Contact List

Two other items are commonly overlooked: your new homeowner's insurance and your contact list. You need to be sure that your new home is properly insured when you take ownership. You also need the following contact numbers to set up accounts for all the services your community provides.

- *Homeowner's insurance* When you schedule an appointment with your mortgage company or other lender, be sure to schedule an appointment with your insurance carrier to complete the necessary paperwork for your new homeowner's insurance policy. This guarantees that your new home will be insured properly from the day you move in. You need to make the necessary arrangements with your homeowner's insurance company at least 14 days before closing. You might want to increase your insurance coverage because of varying mortgage balances, future swimming pools or other improvements, and the increased value of your new home structure. At the time of closing, you're required to have a homeowner's hazard insurance policy equal to at least the total amount of your mortgage.

- *Important contact information* Your realtor or homebuilder will provide all the important contact information for your new home and its surrounding area. Just before closing, you need to call and set up any necessary accounts with your new billing address to ensure there's no interruption in service for the following items:

  - Local power company
  - Telephone
  - Cable TV
  - Water
  - Sewer and trash
  - Fire, police, and ambulance
  - Irrigation (if necessary)
  - Homeowner's association

- *Closing funds* You might be required to bring a cashier's check to the title company when you're scheduled to sign your closing documents. Be sure to call and verify the amount with your title company on the day you're set to close to ensure that your check is issued for the correct amount. If it's incorrect, it could delay your closing. In addition, the title company should be notified early, with frequent reminders, that the final closing statement should be ready three to five days ahead of time for review.

- *Grading and landscaping*   Your new property has been graded according to the approved plans, and these plans are now part of the city or county final inspection. This inspection is required to receive your Certificate of Occupancy (C of O) so that you can move into your new home. In many cases, the plans call for some type of onsite water retention to meet the local municipality's requirement. Onsite water retention allows your property to hold quantities of water during rainfall to minimize potential flooding. Your homebuilder can't make modifications to your yard. As the homeowner, you need to check with your city engineers and/or planning department after close of escrow before attempting to change your lot's contours or grade.

- *Fencing*   If you had a fence constructed to designate your property line, your homebuilder can't guarantee that the fence will be constructed exactly on the property line. Because of grading requirements and lot contours, your fence height might vary. Any changes made to your fencing after you move in are your responsibility, as most cities have restrictions on fence heights. Check with your local building department before making any alterations. Also, if you plan to build block walls or courtyards, a permit might be necessary after the final inspection, or you could be subject to fines.

A Walkthrough Checklist Can Ensure You Look at Everything

The most efficient way to do a final inspection on your new home with your homebuilder is to use a final walkthrough inspection form or checklist. This list includes everything you and your homebuilder need to inspect and discuss. It also gives you the opportunity to write down any items you want repaired and establish a timetable for those repairs with your homebuilder.

Being thorough and observant during the walkthrough is important. Carefully examine all surfaces of counters, fixtures, floors, and walls for possible damage. Sometimes disputes arise because a homebuyer might discover a gouge in a countertop after moving in, and there's no way to prove whether it was caused by the homebuilder's subcontractors or the homebuyer's movers.

At the end of the walkthrough, most homebuilders ask you to sign the checklist to verify that all damage, errors in workmanship, missing items, incomplete items, or other items needing attention have been noted. Now is the time to ask questions and take notes on the answers.

Remember: Every question is a good question. That's how you learn and understand. The walkthrough is your opportunity to agree with your homebuilder on each item as you walk through the house. This way, there's no misunderstanding later, and your new home will be constructed to near perfection.

Take a Look at a Walkthrough List

Here's what a partial sample of a homebuilder's Final Walkthrough Inspection Form (checklist) looks like. You can download the entire walk-through inspection form at http://www.BetterHomesSeminars.com by entering the username and password you received as the owner of this book.

A final walkthrough inspection was performed at (address) for final construction completion, warranty programs, service policy, and homeowner maintenance pertinent to the following items:

Outside: Overall front exterior appearance accepted. ___

Outside: Main water shut-off explained. ___

Outside: Driveway undamaged and accepted. ___

Outside: Electrical breaker panel explained. ___

Outside: Yard cleaned and properly graded; maintenance, landscaping, and watering explained. ___

Outside: Exterior paint accepted. ___

Outside: Doorbell, entry light, and front outside GFI (ground fault interrupt) outlet. ___

Outside: Turn on power, water, and gas. ___

Front: Door and front door latch operational and accepted (maintenance and threshold explained). ___

Front: Entry lights, switches, and plugs operational. ___

Formal Living Room: Windows operating properly, undamaged glass, and proper opening and closing techniques explained. ___

Formal Living Room: Closets, flooring, baseboards, walls, ceiling, doors, and door hardware accepted. ___

Formal Living Room: Light fixtures, switches, and plugs operating properly. ___

Kitchen: Sink undamaged. Faucet is operating properly. Drain stops seal properly. ___

Kitchen: Garbage disposal operates properly. Reset button and use explained. ___

Kitchen: Faucet aerators installed; homeowner shown how to clean and change. ___

Kitchen: All appliances operational free from damage, and warranty information is present. ___

Kitchen: Cabinets free of damage, doors operate properly, and maintenance explained. ___

(And so forth…)

Document any problems you see after you move in. Take photographs and write a description of the problem you're having. Date the document, and send the warranty company and your homebuilder written notification. Mark the 11-month anniversary of your ownership on a calendar so that you don't forget it. Remember: In most cases, your homeowner's warranty expires after one year, and your homebuilder is no longer responsible.

Summary

This chapter has explained what's involved in taking possession of your new home and what responsibilities you have at the time of closing. You've learned how your new home will age over the first year and know what to expect, what's normal, and what needs to be documented, reported, and repaired.

In addition, you've seen why your homebuilder's walkthrough is so important. Taking your time and working with your homebuilder ensure that you get your new home as close to perfect as possible.

23

Home Maintenance: Caring for Your New Home

When you buy a new appliance, such as a TV or a washing machine, usually you have to read the instructions before you understand how to use all its features. Your new home is the same—but with a lot more owner's manuals.

In Chapter 22, "What to Look for Before You Take Possession," you learned to take your time with your homebuilder during the walkthrough and have him show you how to operate the heating and cooling systems, security system, irrigation, central vacuum, swimming pool, circuit breakers, water heater, and other features in your new home. That orientation is important because after you close on your new home, it will be a month or more before you have time to sit down and study all the owner's manuals that come with your new home.

Learning about maintenance responsibilities for your new home is important. Most new homes come with a one-year warranty on workmanship and materials. However, these warranties don't cover problems that develop because of misuse or failure to perform required maintenance. Many homebuilders provide their own booklet or binder explaining common maintenance responsibilities and how to perform them.

Learn How to Care for Your New Materials and Equipment

When you purchase your new home, you won't be familiar with some of its new appliances, equipment, and materials. That's the fun of building your new home with features you never had before. Owner's manuals come in handy to familiarize you with these new features. In addition, your homebuilder might provide something along the lines a "Proper Care and Feeding of Your New Home" document.

This document should include routine maintenance tasks, such as changing the filters in your air-conditioning system, changing the filters in your reverse osmosis (RO) water-purifying system or water softener, or changing the batteries in your new smoke detectors. This document should also include instructions on how to care for your countertops and new wood floors or even your walls, doors, and windows. Here's a partial list of items you need to know how to care for in your new home:

- Countertops
- Cabinets—kitchen and bathroom
- Solid surfaces—laminated plastic, ceramic tile, Royal Stone
- Walls—interior and exterior
- Windows and doors—aluminum framed and natural wood; interior, exterior, and garage doors
- Heating and air-conditioning—filters and registers
- Plumbing—faucets, toilets, bathtubs, drains, water heater, sinks, and garbage disposal
- Septic system—maintenance, pumping, cleanout, and vegetation
- Electrical—circuit breakers, ground fault interrupt (GFI) receptacles, standard outlets, and smoke detectors
- Flooring—resilient, carpet, ceramic, saltillo tile, wood; daily, weekly, and periodic care
- Termite protection

Again, reading and understanding the owner's manuals, warranty information, and maintenance guide your homebuilder provides is important because any damage caused by improper maintenance isn't covered by your homebuilder's warranty. As an example, if a roof leak causes damage to your ceilings because you didn't clean out your new rain gutters, the responsibility for the repairs falls on you.

Take a Look at Some Examples

If you would like a copy of the complete Home Maintenance Instruction Guide, you can download it free from the Web; see the introduction to this book for details. The following excerpted examples give you an idea of what this guide contains:

HOME MAINTENANCE

Your new home should be built with quality materials and workmanship. Many modern conveniences have been included to provide you and your family with pleasant and comfortable living in the years to come. Every home requires regular maintenance and occasional minor repairs. The following additional information will help you keep your new home's appearance, add to its value, and increase your enjoyment of it.

Countertops

Sitting or standing on any countertop is not recommended.

Cabinets

The cabinets in your home should be cleaned with mild cleansers or soap and water. Harsh chemicals and abrasives should not be used. Exposure to high temperatures can damage the finish. Natural wood cabinets should be wiped down periodically with an oil-based, low-gloss furniture polish (such as lemon oil) to prevent wood from drying out during the hot summer months.

Solid Surfaces

Cultured marble: Your new marble surface is designed to give you years of service along with lasting beauty when cared for properly. Proper care will keep it looking new for years to come.

Here's another example of some do's and don'ts:

Royal Stone

- ALWAYS run cool tap water before pouring boiling water into Royal Stone sinks.

- ALWAYS run warm tap water before pouring ice or ice water into Royal Stone sinks.

- ALWAYS use a hot pad or trivet under hot pots or heat-producing appliances.

Get Your Owner's Manuals and Warranties at the Time of Installation

During the construction of your new home, subcontractors install pieces of equipment and appliances at different times. Most pieces of equipment and all appliances come with an owner's manual and a manufacturer's warranty. Make sure you get them all.

This information documents the make and model of each appliance and states who installed them and when. The manuals tell you how to use and maintain your appliances properly but also provide important information if you have a problem with them in the future. You can order a part over the phone, see the wiring diagram, or just provide valuable information to service technicians when scheduling a repair so that they're sure to have the right parts when they arrive.

Remind Your Homebuilder to Save Those Manuals

Homebuilders are busy and have a tendency to miss some details, such as asking subcontractors to leave the owner's manual and warranty information when they install a new piece of equipment or an appliance. When installing something that has accompanying documentation, most subcontractors simply throw it into a kitchen cabinet or drawer—providing you even have kitchen cabinets or drawers at the time. Sometimes manuals and warranty information make it through construction successfully until the final walkthrough, and sometimes they don't. Ask your homebuilder to rescue your documentation and keep it in your file until the walkthrough.

caution If an owner's manual or other documentation is lost, your homebuilder can usually get a copy from the subcontractor or manufacturer. Sometimes, however, getting copies can be difficult and even expensive. If he makes sure to keep these documents for you in a safe place, you're guaranteed to have them at the time of closing.

If an owner's manual or warranty does get lost, however, don't panic. Nearly every manufacturer has all its documentation online. You can download it, read it, and print it, if necessary. You'll be surprised what you can find online, and it's all free.

Get Your List of Subcontractors

When you have the final closing with the title company or at the final walkthrough with your homebuilder, your homebuilder should give you a list of every subcontractor who has worked on your new home. Sometimes it can be quite a list.

When you have a problem, the process for getting warranty work done while your new home is still under warranty is that you notify your homebuilder first, and he inspects the work needing to be done and then instructs you to call the specific subcontractor who performed that work. He doesn't do this because he's handing off the responsibility. He asks you to contact the subcontractor directly because he wants you to be able to schedule the appointment at your convenience. This procedure is much more efficient when you're already in your new home.

Your homebuilder is still responsible for seeing that the work is completed correctly and in a reasonable amount of time. If there are any problems, you can call your homebuilder again, and he'll address any issues you have with his subcontractors.

Subcontractors Warranty Their Work, Too

Your homebuilder and each of his subcontractors warranty their work just as appliance companies warranty their products. Each subcontractor relies on quality of workmanship and materials for his reputation. In my experience, every good subcontractor stands behind the work he has performed and does whatever is possible to correct any problem that comes up.

Remember: You can get more flies with honey than you can with vinegar. Even though your first reaction might be getting angry with a subcontractor because something he did went wrong, he's still the one you have to work with to correct the problem. If you take an attitude to work *with* subcontractors to correct the problem, you'll get a better job done and often something thrown in free.

Summary

This chapter has discussed the importance of proper care and maintenance of your new home and explained how to get help understanding what's involved. You've seen some examples of what a home maintenance guide looks like and discovered why it's important to get all your owner's manuals and warranty information from your homebuilder. Make sure your homebuilder gives you a complete list of all your subcontractors. If something does go wrong with your new home, working with them directly can ensure the problem gets fixed to your satisfaction, but be sure to work with your homebuilder first before you call anyone.

See "Additional Resources" on page 4 for details on how to download a free sample home maintenance outline.

24

The Final Touches

Wow, and that's all there is to it! Your new dream home is now complete. It's almost time for you to celebrate and relax, but there are a few things left to do. Don't worry—you're almost all the way there!

A Few Last-Minute Tasks

There are still a few last-minute tasks you need to make sure have been completed:

- Call the termite company about spraying around your foundation and new landscaping to ensure that your pretreatment certificate and warranty remains valid and you'll be safe from termites.

- Now is a good time to relax in the evenings with a good book—well, maybe a dozen good books, such as your owner's manuals and home maintenance guide. Just read a little each evening to help you learn about all the features of your new home and perhaps even put you to sleep early.

- Follow up with your homeowner's insurance company to make sure you receive your new policy. In most cases, your new home will be worth much more than the home you were living in previously, and if something were to happen, you want to be sure you're covered.

- Don't forget to start up your septic system (if you have one). It's cheap and easy and helps ensure that the system works efficiently—and doing that will keep everyone happy.

- Your construction loan has now been converted to a conventional mortgage. Follow up with your lender to find out when you have to make your first payment, and ask when you should expect to receive your payment booklet. You don't want to start out your new home mortgage with a late payment, especially after taking the time to clean up your credit reports.

- By now, you have gone through your final punch list items, worked with your homebuilder, contacted and scheduled your subcontractors, and had them make any necessary corrections. You new home should be nearly perfect now.

- Now is the time to take a deep breath and start prioritizing and planning your contingency projects. You might want to begin with your new swimming pool or installing an irrigation system, designing window coverings, or planting landscaping.

- Begin thinking about some of the small decorating projects you decided to do yourself, such as faux painting a wall, adding crown molding to the den, wallpapering the master suite, planting some grapevines, or adding a trellis.

- Find a safe place for all your blueprints, designs, spec sheets, and other building documents. They will come in handy if you ever want to build an addition, knock out a wall, insert a window, or just locate a wire, pipe, septic tank lid, or drain cleanout.

- Ask your homebuilder to save any leftover paint he used on your new home. Generally, he can't use it elsewhere. These leftovers give you touch-up paint that matches your existing paint colors. Take a permanent marker and label the cans Living Room, Master Bath, Patio Ceiling, and so forth. This way, you won't have to open every can later or guess. I like to paint a piece of scrap wood with several coats of half the exterior wall (field) color and half the trim

caution *Errors to Avoid* **STOP**

Remember: If you're doing large projects yourself, you should contact your local building department to see whether you're required to have a building permit for that work. Building without a permit can result in being fined, and it might prevent you from being able to sell your home in the future. Again, it's about an ounce of prevention.

tip Remember your homebuilder's suppliers he sent you to for tile, carpet, lighting, and plumbing fixtures with your allowances? Speak with your homebuilder about using these suppliers for future purchases and getting his contractor prices. Most suppliers will honor your homebuilder's prices or slightly higher prices, even though the materials are being sold to you.

color, and then label it. Later, if you lose or throw away the paint cans, you still have the piece of wood. You can bring it to any paint store or home warehouse to have it scanned for a matching color. (I just used my scrap wood today before I began writing this chapter!)

- Put your subcontractor's contact list in a convenient and safe place. You might be using it over the next year to have items repaired. Also, mark your calendar for 11 months from now to schedule your one-year walkthrough or final punch-list items.

- Store your New Home Ideas Workbook in a safe and convenient place so that you have access to all your manufacturers' contact information, model numbers, styles, and installation dates. This information is helpful when it's time to replace a bulb, call a service repair technician, or add a complementary light fixture.

- This is also a good time to read about feng shui so that you can optimize your chi. Now that your new home is finished and you're putting the final touches on your decorating, do it with some feng shui style. This approach is all about using arrangements to allow prosperity and happiness to enter your new home.

- Save all your receipts and records and speak with your tax advisor to see whether you can get any additional tax credits for your construction costs, for building a "green home," for extra insulation, or whatever the government is allowing. Do it now before your advisor gets too busy during tax season.

WHAT'S A GREEN HOME?

Green homes are built as resource-efficient homes. They are very energy efficient, make use of construction materials wisely, and include recycled, renewable, and reused resources. These homes are designed and constructed to be healthy for homeowners, more comfortable, and have lower overhead costs, and they're just good for the planet.

The National Association of Home Builders (NAHB) Research Center (http://www.nahbrc.org) has established three different levels of green homebuilding available to builders who want to use these guidelines to rate their projects: bronze, silver, and gold.

	Bronze	Silver	Gold
Lot Design, preparation, and development	8	10	12
Resource efficiency	44	60	77
Energy efficiency	37	62	100
Water efficiency	6	13	19
Indoor environmental quality	32	54	72
Operation, maintenance, and homeowner education	7	7	9
Global impact	3	5	6

Another resource site on green homes is http://www.energybuilder.com/greenbld.htm.

Releasing the Final Draw to Your Builder

As discussed in Chapter 15, "The Importance of Your Financial Draws," your final draw comes when your new home is between 95% and 100% complete. Approximately 10% of the overall amount of your funds is generally retained in your account until the closing of your new home when you legally take ownership.

Hold Back to Ensure That the Punch List Is Complete

At the final draw, you can hold back these funds to be sure your new home is complete, built to your satisfaction, and constructed without any errors. (This is called a "hold-back.") After you have taken possession of your new home and are satisfied with its construction, you can release the remaining final funds to pay your homebuilder in full.

Please remember to communicate with your homebuilder and coordinate the final payment with him. If there are no major items on your punch list that need repair, I recommend releasing the final funds to your homebuilder so that he can pay his subcontractors and suppliers. By the end of the project, you'll have a good enough relationship with your homebuilder to be able to trust that he'll complete any minor repairs to your satisfaction. Remember: If he doesn't, you can always contact your Registrar of Contractors Office or state contractors licensing agency for resolution.

Enjoy Your New Home!

Now it's time to starting enjoying your new dream home. It's time to go visit your homeowner's association community areas and go to the pool or play some tennis (if applicable). Visit your new malls and other stores in your area. Get familiar with your new local amenities.

After you have had a few good nights' sleep in your new home, you might feel ambitious enough to start thinking about your next project. Do it now while the process is fresh in your mind. This way, it will be easier to compile a list of items and design elements that you couldn't include in this design and have saved for future projects.

When you're ready for your next project, be sure to speak with the lender who handled your loan for this new home. He knows who you are and knows your credit scores. He can also process a new loan, a second mortgage, or a home improvement loan faster and more cheaply than someone new can.

tip
Your homebuilder's subcontractors might be happy to work directly with you when you're ready to make some changes or add-ons or start doing some projects on your wish list that weren't included in your new home's original design. The best people to work on your home are the ones who built it. Also, keep in mind that even though you have worked with those subcontractors before, when you hire them again, always check their pricing on labor and materials. Get bids and compare, as you learned in Chapter 13, "Get Your Own Costs and Compare."

Purchase *Plan a Fabulous Party In No Time*

Now that your new home is finished, it's time to start planning your house-warming party. This is where all your hard work and expense really pay off. You get to share your new home with your family, friends, and co-workers (and even your homebuilder and a few choice subcontractors, if you like).

If you need help planning your house-warming party, here's your next book from Que Publishing to read: *Plan a Fabulous Party In No Time*, by Tamar Love. This book is filled with great tips and tricks that can make your house-warming party as big a success as your new home.

Be sure to check with your bookseller or go to Que Publishing online at http://www.quepublishing.com for other home improvement books, such as *Organize Your Home In No Time*, by Debbie Stanley; *Repair Your Home In No Time*, by Brooke Stoddard; *Speed!: Understanding and Installing Home Networks*, by Michael Wolf; *Absolute Beginner's Guide to Home Automation*, by Mark Soper; and *Organize Your Garage In No Time*, by Barry Izsak.

Last reminder: Please stop by http://www.BetterHomesSeminars.com from time to time, as I'll be adding new items there especially for you. Also, please feel free to email me at any time. I'll be happy to answer any questions I can, and I would love to hear from you about how you Built Your New House In No Time.

Summary

This chapter has given you a checklist for all the tasks you still need to do, even though your new home is complete. You've also reviewed the topic of your homebuilder's last financial draw, when you have to pay your homebuilder to make sure your home is built the way you want it.

This might be a good time for a few thoughts about what your next project might be. Make sure you start this process only after you have had several good nights' sleep in your new home. Above all, relax, look around, enjoy your beautiful new home, and start planning your house-warming party!

Part V

Appendixes

Resources and References

Here is an easy-to-use list of resources and references mentioned throughout the chapters of the book.

The U.S. Census Bureau is a great place to find almost any kind of statistic. This part of the Census Bureau website provides statistics on construction spending:

http://www.census.gov/const/www/c30index.html

The number of licensed realtors registered with the National Association of Realtors (NAR) last spring broke 1,005,785. You can visit the NAR on the web:

http://www.realtor.org/rocms.nsf/Home/ ROHome?OpenDocument

The median price of an existing home in the United States for 2005 was $267,400, according to the National Association of Realtors. This information is also available from the U.S. Census Bureau website:

http://www.census.gov/const/www/ newressalesindex.html

UBuildIt is a building-assist company based in Kirkland, Washington with 104 franchises located throughout the United States:

http://www.ubuildit.com

To learn more about mortgage types and rates and to better understand the lending process, visit PickMyMortgage:

http://www.pickmymortgage.com

The most common credit score is the FICO score, and lenders base their approval on this score. You have three FICO scores, one for each credit bureau, and you can get all three scores from myFICO:

http://www.myfico.com

Under the Consumer Reporting Act, you are entitled to a copy of all the information the three credit agencies have on you:

- *Equifax*—800-685-1111, http://www.equifax.com
- *Experian (formerly TRW)*—888-397-3742, http://www.experian.com
- *TransUnion*—800-888-4213, http://www.transunion.com

The American Arbitration Association (AAA, not to be confused with the American Automobile Association) is a not-for-profit, public service organization committed to resolving disputes through the use of arbitration, mediation, and other voluntary procedures:

http://www.adr.org

The American Arbitration Association wording you need to invoke binding arbitration in your agreements can be found at

http://www.adr.org/sp.asp?id=22297

If you're curious about whether realtors have a code of ethics and standards of practice, you can find the NAR code of ethics at

http://www.realtor.org/mempolweb.nsf/pages/printable2005Code

Here's a typical code of conduct that CitiBank uses:

http://www.citigroup.com/citigroup/corporategovernance/data/codeconduct_en.pdf

The Sarbanes Oxley Act of 2002 mandated the adoption of codes of ethics at publicly traded companies that focuses on corporate ethical behavior, policies, procedures, and practices:

http://www.sarbanes-oxley.com

You'll find information on Continuing Education Credits (CEUs), at the largest governing agency in the U.S., the International Association for Continuing Education and Training in Washington, D.C.:

http://www.iacet.org

Licensing for title agents is running a close second to residential mortgage broker licensing, with the trend strongly suggesting that in a few years, both professions will be regulated:

http://www.schoolofmortgagelending.com

The best way to be sure your potential contractor is licensed, in good standing, and free of professional claims against him is to check with your state's Registrar of Contractors (ROC) or Contractors State License Board. Every state has one:

- California's is http://www.cslb.ca.gov
- Arizona's is http://www.rc.state.az.us
- Nevada's is http://www.nscb.state.nv.us
- Illinois's is http://www.dpr.state.il.us/licenselookup/default.asp

To find your state requirements and websites, go to

http://www.contractors-license.org

Most counties now have a *graphic information system* (*GIS*). If you search the Internet for your county's tax assessor's office, you might find its system. Here's the link for Maricopa County, Arizona:

http://www.maricopa.gov/Assessor/GIS/map.html

When searching the Internet for "House Plans", Google returned more than 39,400 matches, many of which had from 15,000 to 18,000 sets of plans. Here are a few websites:

- *CoolHousePlans.com*—http://www.coolhouseplans.com
- *DreamHomeSource.com*—http://www.dreamhomesource.com
- *HousePlanGuys.com*—http://www.houseplanguys.com
- *HomePlans.com*—http://www.homeplans.com/welcome.asp

Many project plans are available for immediate download after you've purchased them. Because *downloadable project plans* are delivered right to your desktop, you are provided these plans in a PDF file format, which can be opened with Adobe Acrobat Reader free from Adobe at

http://www.adobe.com

If you're set on using an architect, however, you can go back to the Internet to find a discount architect. You can find an architect at

http://www.discountarchitect.com

Two examples of publicly traded production homebuilders are Kaufman and Broad (K&B) and Centex Homes. In 2004, K&B built 31,646 new homes, generating revenues of $7.05 billion. Centex Homes (Home Division) built 30,358 new homes, generating $7.60 billion in annual revenues.

- Kaufman and Broad—http://www.kbhome.com
- Centex Homes—http://www.centex.com

You can also visit the American Society of Interior Designers (ASID), which maintains a database of thousands of professionals across the country. You can call their free referral service at 800-775-ASID:

http://www.asid.org

Another place I go for most personal and business phone numbers is Switchboard. Just type in the category or company name, enter your city and state, and select the surrounding area. In an instant, Switchboard displays a list, starting with the company closest to your home and moving farther out as you go down the list.

http://www.switchboard.com

If you are looking for help with spending wisely, take a look "Helpful Resources for Smart Money Management" at

http://www.smartmoneytips.com

If you want to explore dozens of sample submittal forms, codes, and regulations, you can see the City of Mesa, Arizona's Building and Safety Department forms at

http://www.ci.mesa.az.us/building_safety

More new neighborhoods today are being built as communities governed by their own homeowners' association (HOA) and many are now gated. These neighborhoods are also referred to as *common interest developments (CIDs)* and *planned unit developments (PUDs)*. According to the National Center for Policy Action, approximately one in six people in America, or about 50 million residents, live in a community regulated by a homeowners' association:

http://www.nationalcenter.org

You can find home inspectors by looking in the yellow pages, visiting www.switchboard.com, or contacting the American Society of Home Inspectors (ASHI), which has approximately 1,400 member inspectors nationally, at

http://www.ashi.com

You can also go to InspectAmerica Home Inspections for more information on home inspectors at

http://www.inspectamerica.com

The National Association of Home Builders (NAHB) Research Center has established three different levels of green home building—bronze, silver, and gold—available to builders who want to use these guidelines to rate their projects:

http://www.nahbrc.org

Another resource site on green home building can be found at

http://www.energybuilder.com/greenbld.htm

And of course, for the very best in educational and "How To" books, you must visit Que Publishing at

http://www.quepublishing.com

For more information on home building support documents and the Confidential Contractor's Costs spreadsheets, visit me at

http://www.BetterHomesSeminars.com

And, for more information about me the author, please feel free to visit me at

http://www.LonSafko.com

Index